lustig

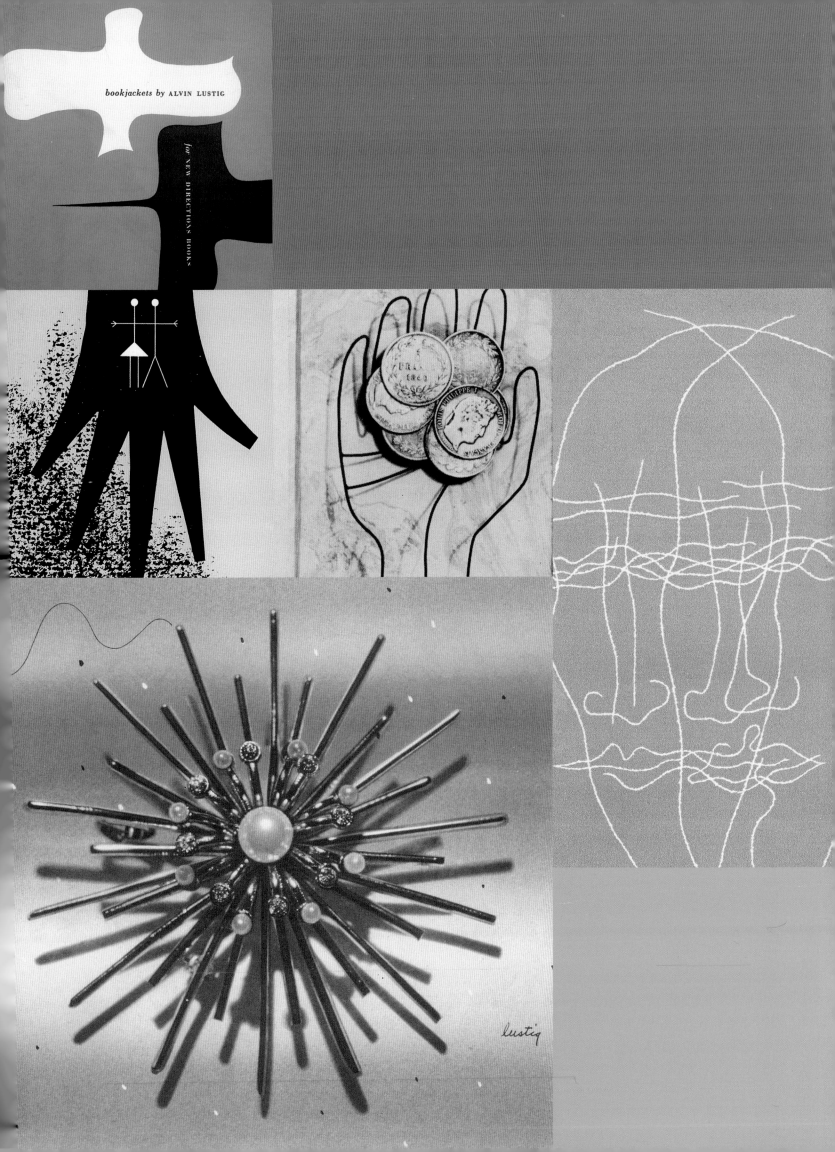

bookjackets by ALVIN LUSTIG

for NEW DIRECTIONS BOOKS

lustig

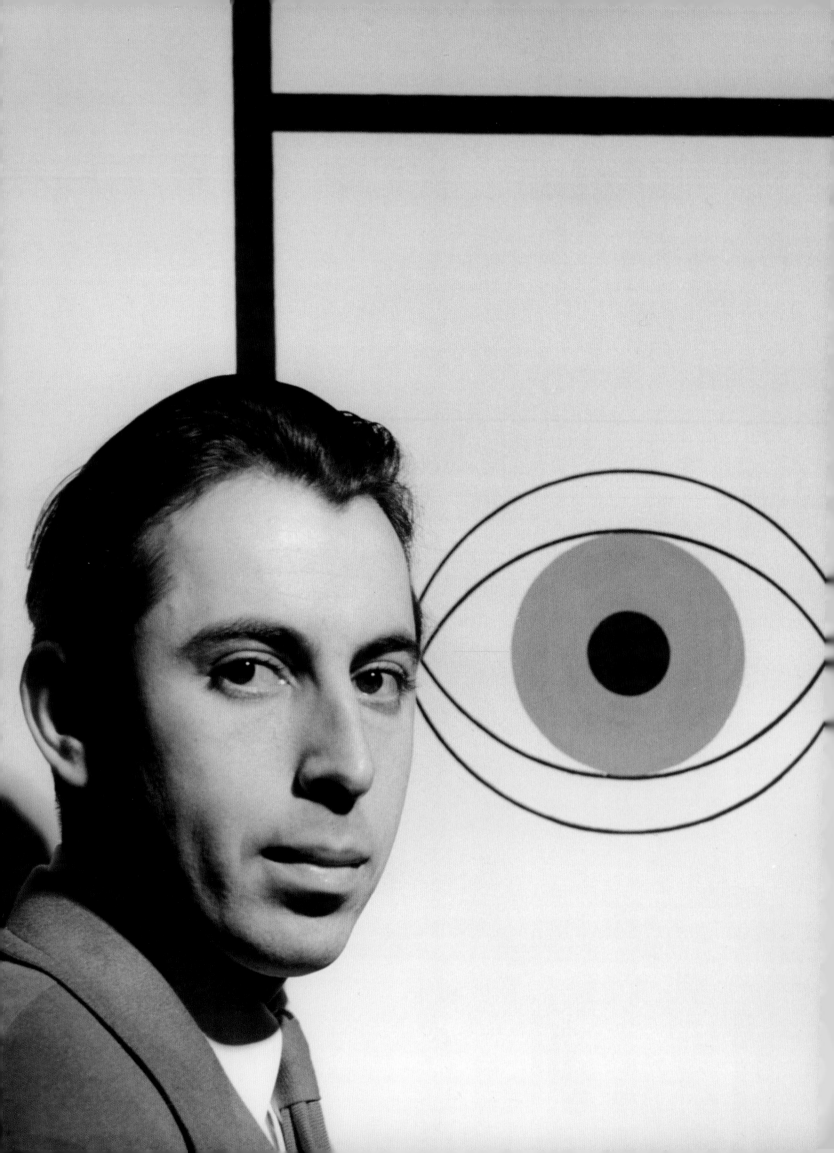

BORN MODERN
The Life and Design of Alvin Lustig

By Steven Heller and Elaine Lustig Cohen

CHRONICLE BOOKS
SAN FRANCISCO

Library of Congress Cataloging-in-Publication Data available.

ISBN: 978-0-8118-6127-4

Manufactured in China.

Art direction and design: Tamar Cohen

Back cover: Alvin Lustig, 1945.
Photograph by Maya Deren.

Endpapers: **Incantation** (fabric came in various colors)
produced by Laverne Originals, 1947.

Title page: Alvin Lustig, c. 1944–45.

10 9 8 7 6 5 4 3 2 1

Chronicle Books LLC
680 Second Street
San Francisco, CA 94107

www.chroniclebooks.com

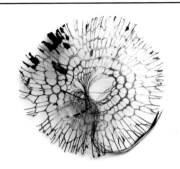

Foreword

The year was 1948: I had just graduated from college and received an appointment to teach art in the Los Angeles public school system. Little did I realize that my life was soon to change forever.

At the opening of a newly formed museum in Beverly Hills, I met a handsome man with intense brown eyes, a sensuous voice, and the most expressive hands I had ever seen. His name was Alvin Lustig. . . . And so began my new journey into the world of design, and into a full life with him.

It is unfortunate that the only portraits remaining of Alvin show him looking reserved and formal—he had a tremendously playful sense of humor and an infectious laugh, but casual photos hardly exist, as we did not own a camera. Alvin believed that if you were always looking through the eye of a camera, you missed the true picture.

Alvin, whose mark on the history of design was established with the covers for the New Directions's New Classic series, was also a remarkable and influential teacher; in fact, he was always the teacher, whether dealing with lover, wife, friend, client, student, or casual acquaintance. After more than fifty years, I can still hear him saying, "Always letter-space caps," "Never use cap italics," "Always use flush-left when writing letters. And place the date last." What was remarkable about this outwardly reserved young man was his tenacity and his absolute confidence in what he wanted to accomplish. He truly believed that all could be realized with the correct visual education.

Everything that Alvin designed possessed a vision that was always very personal and experimental. I once remarked to someone that if you asked him to design a country, the only question he would ask would be, "When would you like it?" His love of form spanned the natural and industrial worlds. Tellingly, the bookshelves in his office displayed seashells, sponges, and a boat propeller. As a true Californian, he also loved cars, and one of his favorite possessions was our new 1948 black convertible Studebaker. Saturday afternoons were spent driving through the hills around Los Angeles, visiting the building sites of new modern homes that were sprouting up everywhere.

I can see him now, sitting at his empty table with a pad of fourteen-by-eleven-inch tracing paper, making pencil sketches: ten or more tiny shorthand images of what his mind's eye was seeing. Alvin's ability to think visually in both two and three dimensions and then eloquently express it verbally certainly helped as his eyesight faded. Alvin's work seems as vital today as it was at the time of his death. My memory is not of him as a "graphic designer," but as an imaginative artist whose warmth and gentleness touched all who knew him.

Elaine Lustig Cohen

Introduction

In the early 1940s, the publisher of New Directions, James Laughlin, commissioned the young graphic designer Alvin Lustig to design covers and jackets for books by Dylan Thomas, Tennessee Williams, Ezra Pound, Henry Miller, F. Scott Fitzgerald, and other literary greats. Laughlin was infatuated with "the young man who was doing 'queer things' with type" and offered Lustig free rein to create a visual persona for his independent publishing house specializing in fiction and poetry. Lustig seized the opportunity and developed a distinct, innovative graphic language combining abstract art and modern typography, conceiving a style that we will call expressionistic Modernism, which was unlike anything seen at that time in the literary marketplace. The jackets made such a strong impact on New Directions's bottom line that Laughlin declared Lustig "an artist who might possess a touch of genius."

Ultimately, Lustig touched the emerging design culture with his many gifts. As a visual form-giver, he became a model for how integral a designer's touch can and should be to the worlds of art and commerce; his influence was palpable. An article in *Interiors* magazine (unsigned) in 1946 lauded, "Alvin Lustig, who has achieved distinction in many fields of design, is a self-made man. Since he is only 31, he has not yet reached the half-way mark in that undertaking . . ."[1] And Claire Imrie predicted in 1952: "You will hear more and more of Alvin Lustig in the next few decades. At thirty-seven he is one of the top ranking book designers and book jacket designers."[2] His numerous solo exhibitions in museums and galleries around the world were double-edged testaments to this foresight. For tragically, two years after Imrie's article, Lustig was blind—and the next year, on December 4, 1955, at the age of forty, he died of the diabetes he had contracted as a teenager (Lustig suffered from Kimmelstiel-Wilson syndrome, for which there is still no cure).

In the decade following Lustig's death, Imrie's prediction did, paradoxically, come true: "A good deal was heard about him," wrote R. Holland Melson, Lustig's former student and an art director at the *New York Times* who edited the only anthology of Lustig's essays. But he added, "One doesn't hear much about him today."[3]

Since Lustig's career ended prematurely, there was little opportunity for him to reach the same professional heights as other contemporary designers who were arguably of the same stature, including Paul Rand, Saul Bass, and Charles and Ray Eames. By the '60s, his accomplishments had faded into the miasma of an as yet unwritten design history. Nonetheless, during the two decades in which he practiced, Lustig threw himself into considerably more varied projects in myriad media than Imrie's modest description suggested. Lustig was the personification of the total designer—a master of interrelated forms and methods—as envisioned by progressive design reformers from William Morris to the Bauhaus masters.

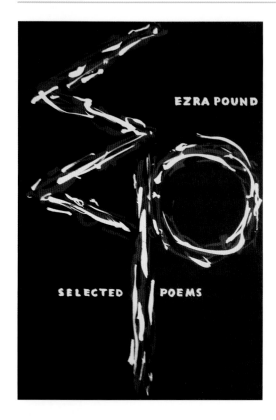

If the heights of professional practice are measured on total output and sheer innovation, then Lustig reached the zenith, even in his short lifetime. The prodigious cross-disciplinary work he produced—from book jackets to a helicopter design, textiles, furniture, magazines, logos, trademarks, sign systems, advertisements, and office and home interiors—equaled the output of others who lived for twenty, thirty, and even forty years longer. The English critic C. F. O. Clarke wrote in a 1948 issue of the Swiss design magazine *Graphis*: "Among present-day attempts to bridge the gulf between 'fine art' and 'applied art,' . . . American designer Alvin Lustig . . . has already established himself as one of the leaders among the group of young American graphic artists who have made it their aim to set up a new and more confident relationship between art and the general public."[4] In notes written for one of his unpublished essays, Lustig said: "Our most creative act at this moment is synthesis. Already we can see the dim outlines of universality that will satisfy our deepest needs. For the artist the primary problem is to find some balance between his own personal creative integrity and still undefined wants of society."[5]

Many of Lustig's projects addressed the social dimension of design and the role of designers. He believed that good design could enhance everyday life, as well as persuade, delight, and entertain an audience. Good design was not always, in fact was rarely, rooted in doggedly familiar or clichéd solutions. And while Lustig did not flagrantly experiment with new form at a client's expense, he took every opportunity to push boundaries to introduce the unfamiliar. Fortunately, he was articulate enough to explain his motives and design solutions without dismaying his benefactors.

Lustig had personal dislikes. He railed against the myopic view of many designers who were stolid commercial artists, slavishly sticking to their niches of expertise. He fervently believed that designers needed to work interdependently in order to have maximum impact on the broader culture, not just the design community. "One of the more severe penalties of over-specialization," he wrote in the *American Institute of Graphic Arts Journal*, "is the lack of nourishing and fertile exchange, which always results from isolation."[6] Where he learned this ethic at a time when most commercial artists wore blinders is not entirely clear, but it certainly did not come from extensive studies or intensive apprenticeships.

His design education was principally informal, and to a large extent his talent was incubated in isolation. His brief stay at Taliesin East, Frank Lloyd Wright's storied studio, was indicative of what would become a continued restlessness. Lustig's hand-typed application letter mailed on April 25, 1935, directly to Wright explains his goal: "My past study has been as an artist and designer, rather than a structural engineer. . . . I studied with Kem Weber [the famed California furniture and industrial designer and architect] at the Art Center School. . . . and while there was little work with architecture, I studied independently the men I admired." Even at that early point in his life, Lustig was harshly critical of traditional practices: "Although my interest in architecture is strong, the interest in the re-uniting of architecture, painting and sculpture is stronger. The dismal museum and degenerate architecture

NIGHTWOOD

djuna barnes

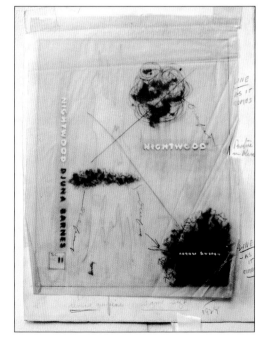

Page 8:
Alvin and Elaine, Los Angeles, 1949.

Page 10:
Alvin Lustig in his office,
Beverly Hills, office 1946.

Opposite:
Ezra Pound's Selected Poems, 1948.
Sketch for unpublished book jacket.

Above:
Nightwood, 1945.
New Directions.

Top and bottom right:
Nightwood, 1945.
Original mechanicals provided to the printer.

succeeding in bring [*sic*] a chaos from which we are just beginning to emerge."

His reason for wanting to study with Wright was a desire for "intense training . . . Consequently I have been studying by myself but the need to work with a master and other students of real purpose is strongly felt."

Lustig's desire seems (in retrospect, of course) to anticipate his untimely death. He deliberately packed his life with work and work-related relationships that would fill many normal lifetimes. His ardent practice of the arts and architecture was manifest in everything from his printing and typesetting business, started when he was in his early twenties, to his complex environmental signage for the first American shopping mall, the Northland Shopping Center in Detroit (see page 173). He took on everything that came his way—or that he could extract from potential clients.

The often reserved young Lustig—by all accounts he was rather shy—was nonetheless never short of chutzpah. He started a design business while attending public school and found that he could amass extracurricular freelance assignments, including invitations and greeting cards, which enabled him to hone his typographic craft and test those proverbial boundaries. In Los Angeles, he rented a studio on West Seventh Street and targeted architects—a group he greatly admired—as clients for his printing and design talents. Although the assignments were for small concerns, his exquisite craft and sophisticated nuance raised the bar on what was called "job" printing. One of his jobs was to design a card for a celebrated bookseller, Jacob Zeitlin, which launched a long friendship. It was Zeitlin who introduced Lustig's work to Ward Ritchie, one of L.A.'s most adventuresome independent publishers.

Thanks again to Zeitlin, Lustig's typographic machinations caught James Laughlin's eyes around this time, and New Directions became an even larger, more expansive laboratory

for him. The sales of New Directions books increased by 300 percent after Lustig started designing the covers because bookshop owners felt more compelled to display them. The impact of these enticing covers on subsequent generations of book cover designers has also been considerable. The painter, photographer, and type manipulator Ed Ruscha cites Lustig's illustrations for New Directions as an influence on his early work, and many contemporary book cover designers have been equally entranced by his rejection of literalism.

Lustig quickly emerged as a key figure in the small California design scene—which was so tightly interconnected that the traditional design specializations between disciplines were routinely blurred. Although Lustig twice abandoned the West Coast for the East Coast, while in Southern California he was a fervent advocate whose early work helped define L.A.'s modern graphic style. He was also a strident defender of California culture. In notes for an essay called "California: The Cultural Frontier," he wrote: "The tendency to consider California nothing but a vast, sun-drenched landscape dotted with buildings the shape of puppy dogs, aging Iowans, orange trees and swimming pools . . ." gives the wrong impression. "How can there be vitality when intellectual activities seem so thinly represented and the mass of people appear to be concerned

Abstract watercolor and ink sketches
for personal experiment, c.1940s.

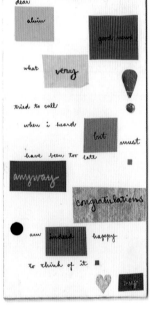

Top:
Alvin and Elaine's wedding day,
December 19, 1948.

Bottom:
Ray Eames's congratulations note
(made as collage) with envelope
sent to the Lustigs, 1948.

Opposite:
Alvin and Elaine, Los Angeles
office, 1949.

primarily with lying in the sun and the general architectural effect suggests a set for a musical comedy that will probably run about a week."[7] He apologized for being harshly negative, but "I think it will strengthen my defense," he added. For Lustig, California fulfilled an American dream—it offered sun, space, air to grow things, and freedom of movement. "The shrunken, domestic scale of the east is too small for us," he added, "and if in the exuberance of our freedom we have committed some rather flagrant errors, be patient; we are still very young." He concluded by suggesting that California is fertile ground for progressive design because, "New ideas when finally accepted are shared by everyone rather than by the small intellectual elite groups that so dominate the east."

Utopian California did, however, have one major problem. There was a paucity of important design work, at least for Lustig, who always lived from hand to mouth. He became a charter member of a very small group (including Saul Bass, Rudolph de Harak, John Follis, and Louis Danziger) called The Los Angeles Society for Contemporary Designers, whose members were frustrated by the dearth of creative vision exhibited by West Coast businesses.

In 1944, he was offered the unique opportunity to direct an experimental design department for *Look* magazine in New York, then one of the top three national weeklies. The dream job abruptly ended in 1946, and he returned to Los Angeles, where he opened a new office and merged graphic design with an expanding emphasis on architecture, furniture, and fabric design.

By the late '40s, when he met and married Elaine Firstenberg, he was certainly on par with Paul Rand, Saul Bass, Herbert Matter, Will Burtin, and others in the design pantheon of American Modernism. His voice was sought after, and his method became a model for a generation of younger designers.

Lustig was ahead of the curve in American design pedagogy, though he was grounded in the Bauhaus method. In a proposal to the University of Georgia titled "A Suggested Plan For An Area of Design Research," he wrote, "This program will concern itself with investigation in design through the

use of materials, techniques and processes. The purpose will be to contribute to the public need for well-designed objects and to the student need for concentrated study in design." His stints at teaching— in California, at the University of Georgia, at Black Mountain College, and finally at Yale—ensured that his ideas were propagated long after he was gone.

Lustig sought to "place more emphasis on research aspects of the stated aims," suggesting an integration of research and practice that has become popular in today's design pedagogy. He was also poised to be a critic of design and designers, which in the small, insular world of graphic and industrial design did not always win friends or elicit warm embraces. In an unpublished essay devoted to type and lettering (c. 1950), an example of his critical voice was bold and stinging: "I cannot help but wince at many of the monstrosities that

are committed in the name of 'modern.' These horrors . . . are committed not only because the ideas and principles of the contemporary movement are misunderstood, but also because the role of tradition is misunderstood."[8] These words prefigure, and are just as strident as, the vociferous design criticism being written today.

In 1951, Josef Albers invited Lustig be a Visiting Critic in Graphic Arts at Yale University. Lustig sought to teach committed students to view graphic design as part of a larger design construct. He produced "a climate in which his students and successors could to some extent realize the kind of design activity he worked so untiringly," wrote R. Holland Melson, "and could in a larger sense alleviate what he termed the 'form blindness that dominates this country.'" Of his teaching and, by extension, his influence on other

designers, Melson noted, "The greatest tribute to his impact as a designer/teacher is that what was once said of him can also be said of those he influenced—they have 'a very high standard of dissatisfaction.'"[9]

Even when his rapidly degenerating eyesight should have incapacitated him, Lustig kept his condition secret so that he could accept more work. When his blindness became evident, he gave a party to announce that it would not keep him from designing. "I was doing some rather fancy faking to carry on," Lustig wrote in a letter to a friend. He developed tricks to stay in control of his work, like dictating typographic and color choices to others in the studio with amazing precision. He would specify colors he wanted by such associations as asking for "the dominant yellow in Van Gogh's sunflowers." In the letter, he explained his ability to design from the darkness this way, "My work has always been visualized in the mind's eye and you probably remember how little sketching or drawing I did working."[10]

"Only at the end, when I knew he could not see the forms evolving on the paper did I realize that his creative instinct was akin to that of the poet or the composer," James Laughlin said in an interview after Lustig died. "The forms took shape in his mind."

It is logical to assume that Lustig was on a mission (some who knew him even spoke of a religious as well as spiritual fervency), not just to succeed at his chosen profession, but to change the definition and perception of that profession. He as much as said so. "The words graphic designer, architect, or industrial designer stick in my throat," he wrote in *Interiors* magazine in 1946, "giving me a sense of limitation, of specialization within the specialty or a relationship to society and form itself that is unsatisfactory and complete. This inadequate set of terms to describe an active life reveals only partially the still undefined nature of the designer."[11]

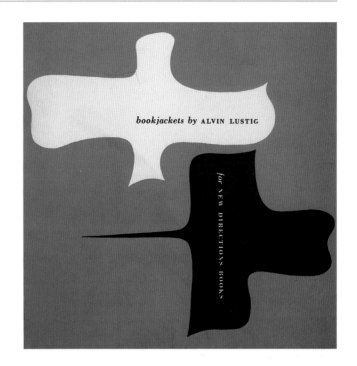

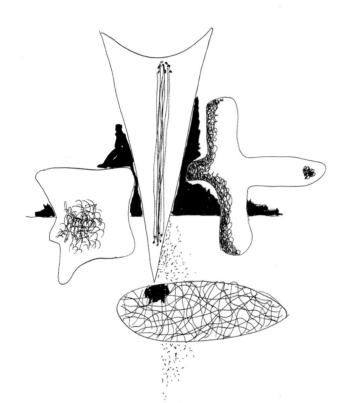

Opposite:
Alvin and Elaine, Los Angeles
office, 1949.

This page, clockwise from top left:
Sketch for personal experiment in
black ink, 1940s.

Bookjackets by Alvin Lustig, 1947.
Cover for The Gotham Book Mart
Press collection of printer's overruns
of jackets.

Sketch for fabric design in black ink
(never produced), 1940s.

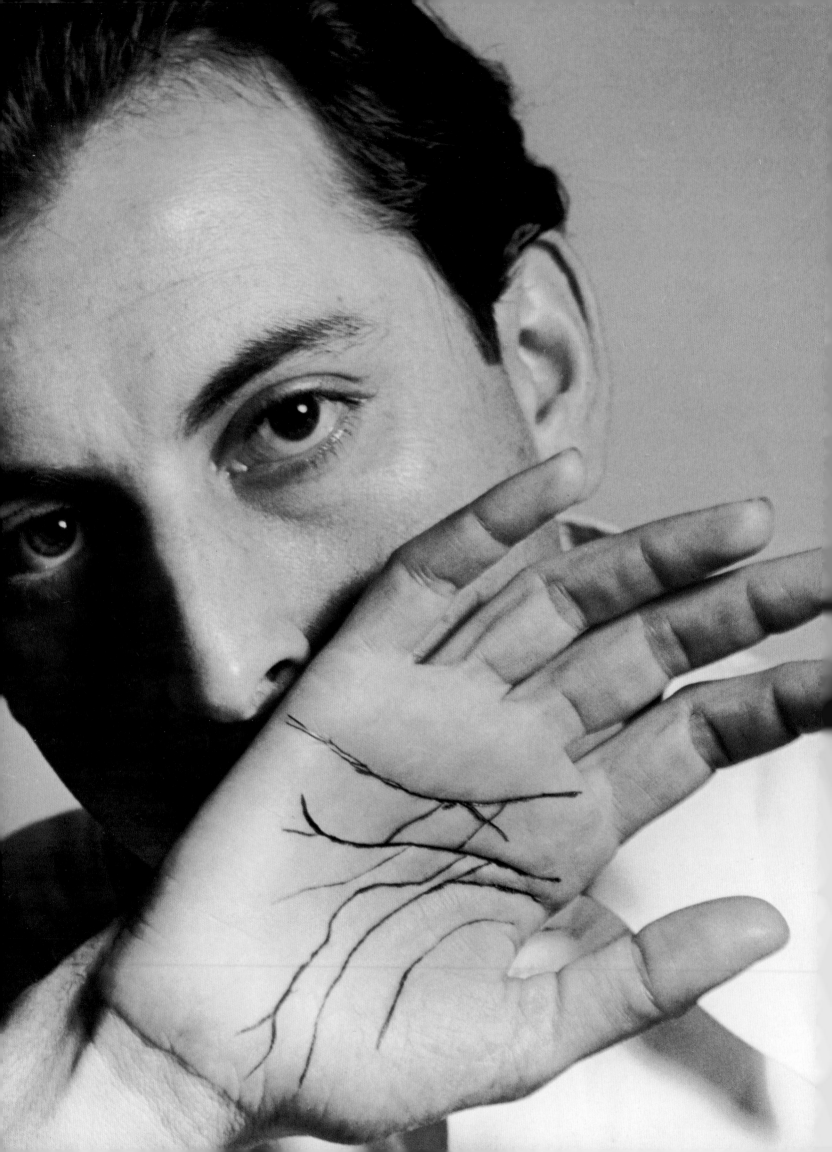

BORN MODERN
The Magic Years

NATURE NOT NURTURE

Alvin Lustig was a design prodigy. His first published illustration appeared on the May 1933 cover of *Touring Topics*, a monthly magazine sent to members of the Automobile Club of Southern California. He was just eighteen when the editors bought his unsolicited cover design. They also let him "talk his way into" a job as the magazine's art director. He had never been an art director or any other kind of director. With only a high school education and no practical experience, he was given an estimable title that would have looked good on any veteran designer's résumé. What was it about him that earned other people's confidence? "He had a wonderful sense of humor with an infectious laugh," his wife, Elaine Lustig Cohen, said later. He also had hubris that shone through his reserved demeanor.

The illustration for *Touring Topics*, which looked much like a wallpaper swatch with its repetitive stylized pattern of a touring car driving past palm trees and snow-capped mountains, was consistent with the dominant *art moderne* graphic style of the day. Yet it was so masterfully rendered and professionally polished that it is astonishing that an adolescent could do such work. Even his signature—Alvin Lustig—stacked on two lines, lettered with the confidence of a seasoned cartoonist-illustrator, belied his youth. The cover, with its deco shading and highlights, clearly required considerable skill to execute. Where did he acquire this aptitude, talent, and expertise?

Little in Lustig's family history indicated a future as an exceptional artist. Neither of his parents seems to have been artistic. Alvin's father, Harry Lustig, was born on July 7, 1881, in Millersburg, Ohio, to Austrian immigrants, Elias and Rige Spere Lustig. (In German, *lustig* means "merrily" or "playfully.") Harry grew up in a poor section of Youngstown, Ohio, where he was friends with the Warner brothers (née Wanskolaser), sons of a Polish immigrant merchant who later became Hollywood moguls with the motion picture studio that bore their anglicized name. In his twenties, Harry moved to Denver, Colorado, where he met his future wife Jeanette Schamus. Jeanette was born in Russia (date unknown, possibly in Odessa), then moved with her parents, Samuel, a butcher, and Sarah Fishel Schamus, to Denver, where she attended school. She married Harry in 1914. A year later, Alvin was born. In 1920, the family moved to Los Angeles so that Harry could take a job as a salesman for Metro Pictures. In 1922, Alvin's sister, Sarabelle was born. (She later changed her name to Susan.) In 1923, Metro merged with the Goldwyn Company and Louis B. Mayer to form MGM. Given a surfeit of salesmen after the merger, Harry was let go. Meanwhile, the Warner brothers, who had expanded from a nickelodeon business into a feature film studio, offered their childhood friend a job as manager of distribution at Warner Bros. Pictures. Now with a substantial salary, the Lustigs bought a comfortable house on Wellington Road.

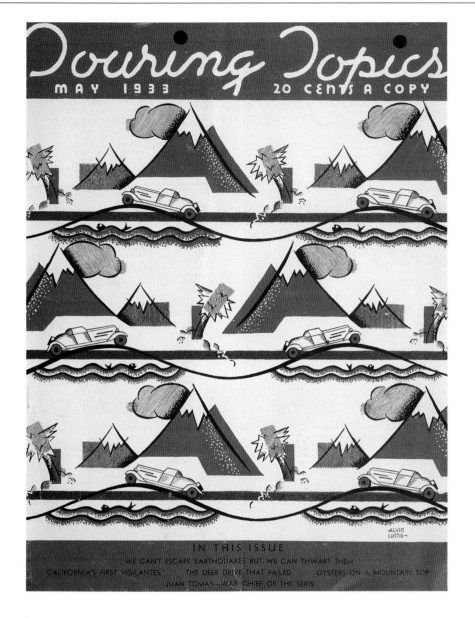

Page 20:
Alvin Lustig, c. 1944–45.

Above:
Touring Topics, May 1933.
Magazine cover for the Automobile
Club of Southern California.

Top right:
Alvin Lustig, age 3, Los Angeles.

Bottom right:
Alvin Lustig, age 12, Los Angeles.

Top:
Alvin, age 10, and younger sister,
Susan, Los Angeles, 1920s.

Bottom:
Alvin performing sleight of hand for
his sister, Los Angeles, 1920s.

Alvin's parents had been raised in traditional Jewish families, but their own family was not religiously observant. Alvin was never given a bar mitzvah (although he toyed with having one when he was an adult). Curiously, his mother flirted with Christian Science—perhaps as a way of coping with Alvin's ultimately fatal juvenile diabetes, diagnosed when he was a teenager, or for other more spiritual reasons—but this flirtation did not influence the rest of the family. However, from the age of fifteen to eighteen Alvin attended the Christian Science church. "Frankly, I abandoned it," he wrote to a friend in 1954, "not because I do not believe that spiritual power takes precedence over physical, but because I believe that the relationship between these two forces is considerably more dynamic and subtle than the teachings offered."[12]

The Lustigs did, however, donate to a motion picture industry fund for Jews escaping the Nazis. By the late '40s, Alvin, who had not served in the armed forces during World War II, toyed with the idea of moving to Israel, more out of a sense that good design could make a significant difference in the future of this new nation than for any religious reason. (Nonetheless, the Los Angeles printer and publisher Ward Ritchie notes in an essay titled "Fine Printing: The Los Angeles Tradition" that, around age twenty-two, Lustig was "mesmerized by the story of Christ, which he transferred to his own life. We talked about this. He quite honestly believed at that time that he could be the savior of our civilization. He thought he might even be able to do it through graphics."[13])

When he was ten, Alvin's parents enrolled him in a private art school in Los Angeles. According to David Davies, a printer who in 1983 wrote a brief biography of Lustig culled from various firsthand interviews with friends and family (though he died before finishing and publishing the manuscript), Lustig was not enthusiastic about taking the class, which emphasized pedantic drawing techniques. "On his first Saturday he was handed a box of pastels and told to copy the flowers in a bowl," Davies noted. "He performed the task satisfactorily, but without fervor, his interests being in show business rather than horticulture."[14] Davies was referring to Lustig's nascent interest in puppetry. At this time, Alvin started making puppets and mounting puppet shows in miniature theaters that he constructed. From this, it was clear to his mother that he had a gift worth cultivating.

In 1929, Lustig entered Los Angeles High School, on Olympic Boulevard, not far from his home. His interest in show business continued, but by this time he had become devoted to magic. Floyd G. Thayer, a manufacturer of magic props and illusions based in downtown Los Angeles, befriended Lustig and introduced him to other magicians during regular Saturday visits. Through these acquaintances, he was invited to become a member of the Society of American Magicians and the International Brotherhood of Magicians. As Lustig's proficiency increased, "his fame spread throughout the public school world," wrote Davies, "or at least the Los Angeles segment of it." He performed at so many shows at local grammar and high schools that his mother became worried that the stress would aggravate his diabetic condition. Davies reported that she wrote to the high school principal asking that his performances be "curtailed, if not eliminated." Lustig's bookings were indeed reduced to those at his own school, including a senior year show that he staged with all the magician's trappings— rabbits, pigeons, and six assistants. "His chief, and most beautiful assistant, the girl he sawed in half, was Marjorie Reynolds," wrote Davies. She was later featured in forty movies, including starring roles in *Holiday Inn* with Bing Crosby and *Ministry of Fear* with Ray Milland, and she costarred as the wife in the '50s television series *The Life of Reilly* with William Bendix.

THE MAGIC OF DESIGN

Magic eventually took a backseat to the less strenuous but no less intense fields of graphic design and typography, which Lustig picked up in large part on his own. Aimee Bourdieu, Lustig's high school art teacher, was, however, influential in stimulating his interest in applied art—particularly in advertising posters. She was a modernistic painter who was "scoffed at by all the other members of the faculty," Lustig wrote in his essay "Design, A Process of Teaching" in *Collected Writings*, for her fervent interest in contemporary art and its relationship to design. Lustig was struck by this exposure, "and from that moment my way of seeing was transformed,"[15] he added. Influence and passion trigger different responses. In Lustig's case, his graphics career began with the design of sophisticated posters for his own magic performances. In a burst of creative energy, he also redecorated his L-shaped room in his family's home. (Interior design reemerges throughout his creative life.) Neighbors and strangers came from blocks around to see how he repainted the walls black, white, and rust in a neighborhood "where the favored color was sure-shot taupe," added Davies.[16]

Upon graduating from Los Angeles High School, Lustig assumed the short-lived art directorship of *Westways*. It is unclear what he actually did at the magazine, since art direction was a variegated, often undefined job then (as it is sometimes today), but all indications point to his quickly losing interest in it. He was what today is called a multitasker. In 1933, he also enrolled in a printing class with Richard Hoffman, a fine-press printer, and Harry Koblick, another art teacher with whom he became good friends. Lustig's goal was to open a printing and design business where he could be expressive and teach others letterpress printing. In 1934, he entered Art Center School in Los Angeles—the next step in his ad hoc design education and first foray into architecture. At Art Center, Frank Lloyd Wright was one of the oft-quoted deities. Lustig made his mind up to study at the master's feet. In 1935, at the age of twenty, he went to Taliesin in Wisconsin, where he stayed for three months. "He believed the brochure which described the various workshops. Of course, nothing existed and they mostly fed the pigs on the grounds," wrote Elaine Lustig Cohen. "Alvin could not stand the atmosphere and ran away in the middle of the night after a short stay."[17] One good thing did happen, however—Lustig met another transient Taliesin fellow, Edgar Kaufmann Jr., the son of the Pittsburgh department store magnet who convinced his father to build Wright's design for the epic Fallingwater home in 1936

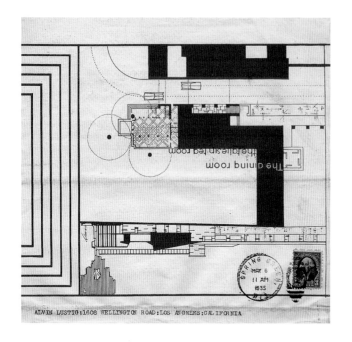

ALVIN LUSTIG:1608 WELLINGTON ROAD:LOS ANGELES:CALIFORNIA

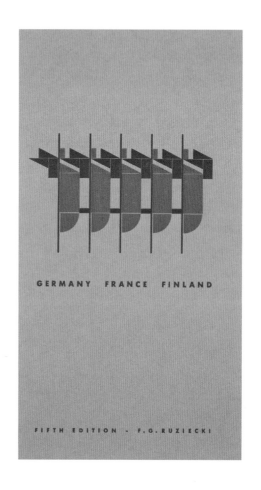

GERMANY   FRANCE   FINLAND

FIFTH EDITION · F.G.RUZIECKI

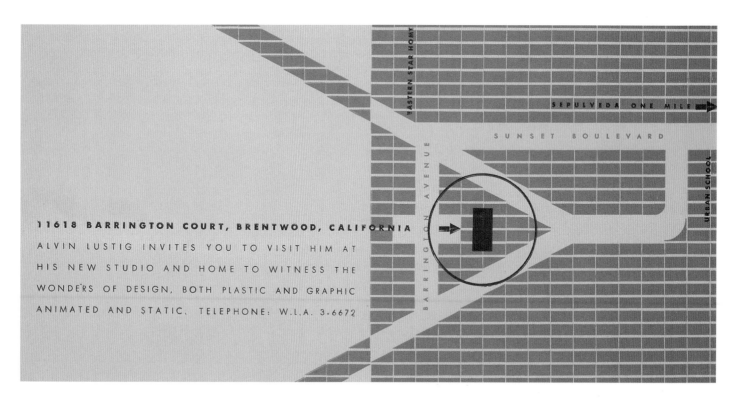

11618 BARRINGTON COURT, BRENTWOOD, CALIFORNIA

ALVIN LUSTIG INVITES YOU TO VISIT HIM AT
HIS NEW STUDIO AND HOME TO WITNESS THE
WONDERS OF DESIGN, BOTH PLASTIC AND GRAPHIC
ANIMATED AND STATIC. TELEPHONE: W.L.A. 3·6672

(Kaufmann worked on the interior specifications). Lustig remained lifelong friends with Kaufmann, who was also a significant modern art collector and one of the forces behind MoMA's "Good Design" exhibition of 1944–56.

Lustig was depressed during his stay with Wright, and not shy about saying so in a frank letter to the master. He felt that his creativity was being destroyed because he was allowed to do things only the "Wright way." After obtaining his "freedom" from the Fellowship in 1936, the twenty-one-year-old returned to Los Angeles and attended Art Center for a year. That same year, Harry Lustig died, and Alvin faced the prospect of complete financial self-reliance. After setting up his own studio (one of many that he designed), he went about soliciting work. Targeting architects, with whom he felt some affinity, he sought to render simple projects like letterheads and business cards, but commissions were few and far between. For a time, Davies noted, "he existed on oatmeal porridge, eaten three times a day, and there were times when he had no idea where his next box of Quaker Oats would come from."[18] While his freelance career did not have an auspicious beginning, Lustig was nonetheless making contacts that would provide opportunities later. The most important solicitation during that early period was when he ventured into the bookshop of Jacob Zeitlin, whose first store on West Sixth Street was designed by Wright himself. Zeitlin commissioned Lustig to design a Christmas card, which was printed by Harry "Ward" Ritchie, a bookbinder and printer who ran a highly admired private press between 1932 and 1974 (and helped launch what Zeitlin called a "small renaissance" in the California style of book design). Zeitlin's shop, like the storied Gotham Bookstore in New York, was a mecca for many of Los Angeles's literati and designers of all kinds. Thanks to the well-connected Zeitlin, Lustig received many of his early significant California commissions. The printer Ward Ritchie recalled that when he first met Lustig, "He was a dark-haired ascetic, slender and handsome fellow, very articulate and dedicated." Ritchie initially met Lustig in his studio "up the stairs and down a dingy hall of a store building on Seventh Street."[19] He had freshly painted it and, with very inexpensive and simple

Opposite top:
The Taliesin Fellowship, 1935.
Promotional brochure sent to Alvin.

Opposite middle:
Stamps of Germany, France, Finland, 1939.
Catalog using type case geometric shapes.

Opposite bottom:
11618 Barrington Court, late 1930s.
Announcement for Lustig's new studio in Brentwood.

Above:
Classical study, lithograph, by Lustig, c. 1930.

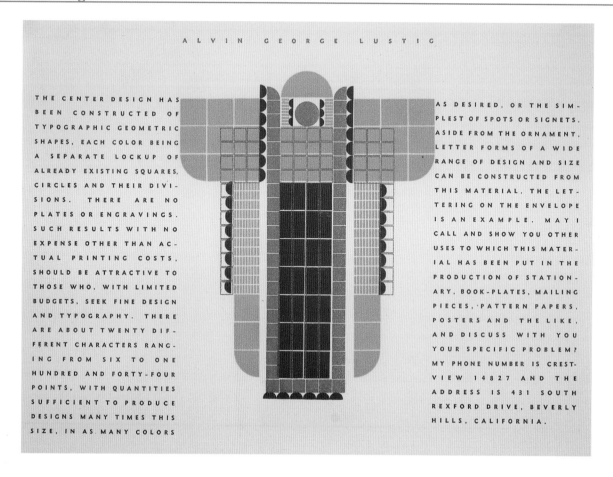

ALVIN GEORGE LUSTIG

THE CENTER DESIGN HAS BEEN CONSTRUCTED OF TYPOGRAPHIC GEOMETRIC SHAPES, EACH COLOR BEING A SEPARATE LOCKUP OF ALREADY EXISTING SQUARES, CIRCLES AND THEIR DIVISIONS. THERE ARE NO PLATES OR ENGRAVINGS. SUCH RESULTS WITH NO EXPENSE OTHER THAN ACTUAL PRINTING COSTS, SHOULD BE ATTRACTIVE TO THOSE WHO, WITH LIMITED BUDGETS, SEEK FINE DESIGN AND TYPOGRAPHY. THERE ARE ABOUT TWENTY DIFFERENT CHARACTERS RANGING FROM SIX TO ONE HUNDRED AND FORTY-FOUR POINTS, WITH QUANTITIES SUFFICIENT TO PRODUCE DESIGNS MANY TIMES THIS SIZE, IN AS MANY COLORS AS DESIRED, OR THE SIMPLEST OF SPOTS OR SIGNETS. ASIDE FROM THE ORNAMENT, LETTER FORMS OF A WIDE RANGE OF DESIGN AND SIZE CAN BE CONSTRUCTED FROM THIS MATERIAL. THE LETTERING ON THE ENVELOPE IS AN EXAMPLE. MAY I CALL AND SHOW YOU OTHER USES TO WHICH THIS MATERIAL HAS BEEN PUT IN THE PRODUCTION OF STATIONARY, BOOK-PLATES, MAILING PIECES, PATTERN PAPERS, POSTERS AND THE LIKE, AND DISCUSS WITH YOU YOUR SPECIFIC PROBLEM? MY PHONE NUMBER IS CRESTVIEW 14827 AND THE ADDRESS IS 431 SOUTH REXFORD DRIVE, BEVERLY HILLS, CALIFORNIA.

furniture, made the space "so attractive that the landlord on seeing it decided he wasn't getting enough rent." Lustig was understandably irritated by being unfairly treated and decided to move out. "Alvin's artistry was his undoing," Ritchie noted, so he took it upon himself to "come to the rescue" by giving him room in his own office. Lustig moved the heavy cases of geometric printing ornaments he was using to construct graphic ornamentation and his fonts of sans serif type into Ritchie's cramped office. "In one obscure corner he kept a desk he had designed to contain three or four drawers of ornaments and a font or so of type. He spent a couple of years there designing bits and pieces for his clients, and we would print them for him," said Ward. In exchange for the office space, Lustig designed announcements and other printed pieces for The Ward Ritchie Press when needed. True to form, he christened his new space by redesigning the front office. The following weekend, Ward Ritchie wrote in a letter to Davies, Ritchie "repainted the renovated office."

"His creative genius for the next few years was directed with an almost messianic intensity toward creating the ultimate in design through color and arrangement of geometric typographical material. And it is doubtful if anyone ever will even approach his achievements in this special field," wrote Ritchie.[20] Among other projects, Lustig created typographic announcements for the Rounce and Coffin Club, to which Ritchie and his partner Gregg Anderson belonged. He also designed announcements for the Stendahl Art Gallery. Stendahl dealt in modern and pre-Columbian art, and the latter held quite an allure for Lustig and became a leitmotif in his design. Stendahl lived on Hillside Avenue next door to Walter Arensberg, the art collector and critic; this connection was beneficial to Lustig, for Arensberg became another significant influence in young Lustig's unorthodox education.

PAINSTAKING PRECISION

Lustig attracted other clients, mostly architects for whom he designed brochures. "He was constantly in and out of the shop soliciting orders, and then returning to compose his striking designs from printers' ornaments," wrote Davies.[21] These signature type case constructions, while reminiscent of earlier Russian Constructivist compositions, were

NUMBER 11 JULY 1940

BOHEMIAN LIFE

AS SEEN BY SAVARIN ST. SURE

PUBLISHED BY BOHEMIAN DISTRIBUTING CO. 2254 EAST FORTY-NINTH STREET LOS ANGELES

decidedly novel in the arena of ornamental designs being done in the United States. They required painstaking precision, but for Lustig it was worth the trouble. It was at this time that Lustig designed typographical decorations (or headpieces) for William Van Wyck's *Robinson Jeffers* (1938) (see pg. 36) and Alfred Young Fisher's *The Ghost in the Underblows* (1940) (see pgs. 43–45). The second book was known for its hypnotic black and red abstract type case designs, which implied a sense of motion and echoed the avant-garde of the '20s.

Lustig didn't go into business to smash typographic rules, but he was not shy about expressing himself in ways that were counter to prevailing typographic trends. In the essay "Personal Notes on Design" in *Selected Writings*, Lustig recalled a lunch organized by Ritchie where he was seated next to an unnamed printer/designer (according to Davies, it was probably Frederic W. Goudy): "We had a vague, pleasant conversation," wrote Lustig, "and I could see that he was saying to himself, 'Isn't it nice that such intelligent young men are attracted to the art of printing.' But at one point during the luncheon, someone mentioned the fact that I was

the designer of a certain book [*The Ghost in the Underblows*] Ritchie had shown to the honored guest earlier. This book was very 'modern' and broke many of the rules of classic typography. The effect of this announcement was frightening. The distinguished visitor's face went white, and he stared at me as though he had just realized that I had leprosy. There was no further conversation."[22]

In 1940, twenty-five-year-old Lustig was more than halfway through his short life, and his career was taking off. The horizon was bright; the field was his to conquer. He was a big shot in the small California modern design realm. He gave up his cramped desk space at Ward Ritchie's shop for his own

Opposite:
Alvin George Lustig, early 1940s.
Announcement for Lustig's Beverly Hills studio:
It reads in part, "for those who, with limited
budgets, seek fine design and typography."

Above:
Bohemian Life, July 1940.
An epicurian newsletter about food
and wine.

studio in Barrington Court in Brentwood. He moved his type cases and designed his own elegantly simple letterhead. He designed letterheads and booklets for clients, experimented with abstract motion pictures, and pushed his boundaries by designing prefabricated furniture and modular houses. Since his studio was not large enough to allow him to pull proofs, he worked out a deal with the printing instructor at Beverly Hills High School to use its letterpress in return for designing commencement programs using his metal type ornamental method—these programs were doubtless unmatched by any other high school in the United States. He made a dramatic impression in the corridors of Beverly Hills High. "He wore a cloak," recalled a former student, Lucien Marquis, "an appendage which would cause no comment in Beverly Hills."

Lustig's short life precludes measuring his achievements by the numbers on a calendar or defining neat periods or epochs in his career. Lustig's many and varied disciplines intersect in time and space and take place on both East and West Coasts. His accomplishments and the variety of his output after 1940 are incredible. The following chapters, which are arranged generally according to discipline, describe his groundbreaking career.

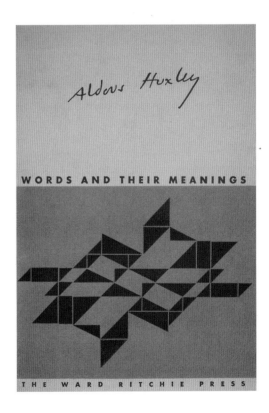

•

Opposite:

Cartoon pencil doodles, 1940s.

•

Top right:

Personal greeting card for gallery

owner Alfred Stendahl, 1940.

Bottom right:

Words and Their Meanings, 1940.

Book binding and interior design

published by Ward Ritchie Press.

PRACTICING MODERN
Life in Print

PRINT MAN

When he began designing book jackets in the late 1930s, Alvin Lustig retained as much overall control as possible, which was not at all the standard operating procedure in the publishing industry. Jacket designers were not usually afforded much freedom; their role was often an afterthought. In fact, at its inception in London in the mid-nineteenth century, the dust jacket was purely utilitarian. Its intent was to protect leather bookbinding from soot, grime, and other corrosive pollution of the Industrial Revolution. Small windows were cut out of the jacket to display the title and author's name, and only at the turn of the century were graphics used to promote and illustrate a book's contents. By the '20s and '30s, some jackets (and ultimately paperback covers) evolved into arty mini-posters. Yet they were routinely removed and discarded before the book was placed on a bookshelf. The designer of the text pages and binding was rarely the designer of the jacket—purists celebrated the former as a craftsman, while the latter was disparaged as a "commercial artist," or advertising hack. Lustig's publishing patrons—for patrons rather than clients are what they were—ceded him control because they realized that he was an artist and the jacket was, well, his canvas.

Lustig lived up to the promise. He developed various original manners and styles. Yet underpinning it all was the fact that he was a card-carrying Modernist rooted in the ethos of the twentieth century European avant-garde. Other contemporary American designers from the late '30s and into the early '60s were similarly inspired—E. McKnight Kauffer, Paul Rand, George Giusti, and Leo Lionni established models for modern book jacket and cover design. But Lustig challenged conventions in ways that were form defining and distinct. He was fluent in the language of surrealistic iconography and symbolic abstraction. He demanded that readers decipher various visual signs and clues, and he played sly pictorial games with their perceptions. Importantly, he also combined modern art with folk and primitive art, forging this hybrid into a contemporary graphic language.

Today Lustig's typography and imagery are as engaging as they were when he first created them—his work defied chronological categorization then, and still does. When comparing his early to later design, it is difficult to date a dust jacket. Lustig's jackets (indeed all his print work) were monuments of ingenuity and objects of aesthetic pleasure. But he never wanted graphics to define him entirely and was adamant about his role in the larger design world. "Too many people still think of me as a graphic designer," Lustig opined to a friend. "Of course I realize the greatest volume of my work has been graphic but I am seeking to change that balance."[23] Which he did by tackling all manner of two- and three-dimensional design. Still, his most

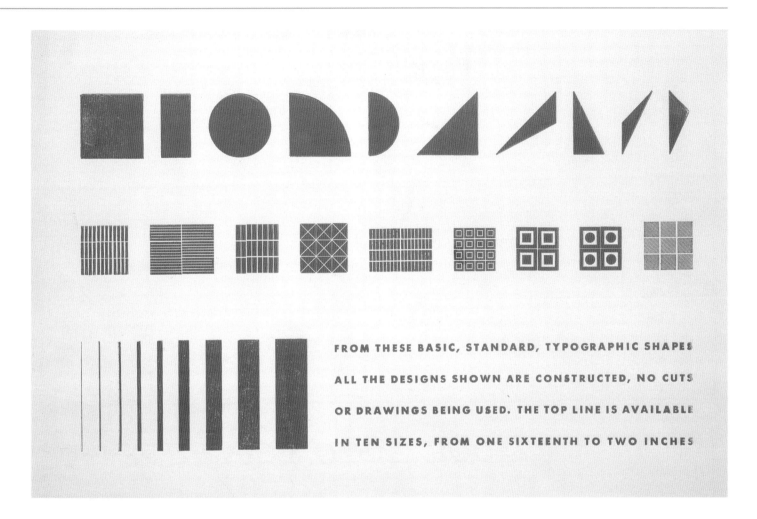

FROM THESE BASIC, STANDARD, TYPOGRAPHIC SHAPES ALL THE DESIGNS SHOWN ARE CONSTRUCTED, NO CUTS OR DRAWINGS BEING USED. THE TOP LINE IS AVAILABLE IN TEN SIZES, FROM ONE SIXTEENTH TO TWO INCHES

Page 32
Alvin Lustig, Los Angeles office, 1949.

Top:
Type case shapes specimen page, late 1930s.

Middle and bottom:
Euclid A New Type, late 1930s.
Two type experiments that led to the design
of the masthead for *Arts & Architecture*
magazine.

ELEMENTS OF TYPOGRAPHY
a summer course with **ALVIN LUSTIG**

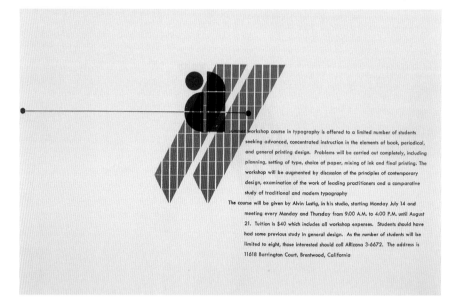

Summer workshop course in typography is offered to a limited number of students seeking advanced, concentrated instruction in the elements of book, periodical, and general printing design. Problems will be carried out completely, including planning, setting of type, choice of paper, mixing of ink and final printing. The workshop will be augmented by discussion of the principles of contemporary design, examination of the work of leading practitioners and a comparative study of traditional and modern typography

The course will be given by Alvin Lustig, in his studio, starting Monday July 14 and meeting every Monday and Thursday from 9:00 A.M. to 4:00 P.M. until August 21. Tuition is $40 which includes all workshop expenses. Students should have had some previous study in general design. As the number of students will be limited to eight, those interested should call ARizona 3-6672. The address is 11618 Barrington Court, Brentwood, California

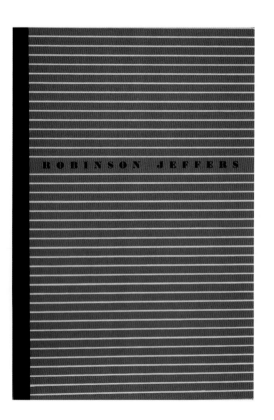

believes him to be, why doesn't he seek self-destruction? The answer is obvious. There are compensations for man's lack of decency and Jeffers has unified them in the grandeur of nature. An eyeful of sky, a lungful of the sea's salty air, a hawk wheeling in the blue empyrean, the silhouette of a mountain against a dawning or an evening sky, the undulations of a field of grain, the quivering activities of wild life, the dash of surf against rocks—all of these console us for the shortcomings of man.

We lesser mortals crawl about on our bellies with our eyes glued to the dust, forever seeking subterfuges, the sophistries of human palaver, the pleasures of the fleshpots, the mumbo-jumbo of creeds, the satisfying

10

of a will to power and all of the mundane trivia, the whiles this veri-poet sits on his rock and gazes bare-eyed at the sun. Deep within the heart of him he knows that man is not worth the gunpowder to blast him from the earth, a thing that he is making a creditable attempt to do at present.

We may bawl all of the platitudes we like concerning the goodness of man, but one war, such as was the great war, discounts all of man's goodness to date. Man will spawn and create future generations to behave as he has always behaved. The small soul will blind itself to all of this and will continue to deceive itself in mouthings that have nothing to do with the words that spring from the heart of a veri-poet.

11

Top left and right:
Elements of Typography: A Summer Course with Alvin Lustig, late 1930s.
Brochure cover and inside spread.

Bottom left and right:
Robinson Jeffers, 1938.
Book binding and inside spread.

Opposite top:
New Year's card, late 1930s.
Designed for Jacob Zeitlin.

Opposite bottom:
Joyous Holiday Season, late 1930s.
Greeting card.

enduring contribution to design and popular culture is graphic design, most notably the book jackets and covers for Ward Ritchie Press, New Directions, Alfred A. Knopf, Noonday, Meridian, and a sprinkling of other publishers. These jackets informed his nonbook work, including magazines and journals, brochures and catalogs, advertisements and promotions, trademarks and logos, and various pieces of ephemera. So it is through graphic design that the door to Lustig's talent is opened.

METAL MAN

Lustig experimented alternately with metal type constructions, photographic manipulations, collage and montage layering, expressionist and abstract scribbling, and modern and even proto-postmodern typographies. Each method left its mark on the form and style of the moment and also left lasting traces. Lustig's employ of vintage type prefigured the revivalist trends in late twentieth- and early twenty-first-century graphic design. While he refused to be pigeonholed—and said that he did not want to be thought of as another graphic designer like Rand and Kauffer—he wrote: "Not that I deny my relationship to them in many ways, but my aims are wider, and I hope, deeper."[24] Paradoxically, his less ephemeral designs—interiors, furniture, and textiles—have been more historically overlooked than his impressive print oeuvre, which survived in multiples and editions.

Lustig did not view himself as a stylist or decorator—yet he was both and more. In the print realm, his copious application of type case slugs, cuts, and dingbats was the beginning of a distinctive Lustig style. In 1939, he produced a specimen sheet of metal ornaments used to advertise his typographical services (and style) and described it this way: "From these basic, standard typographic shapes all the designs shown are constructed, no cuts or drawings being used." The practice of creating ornament and borders from metal was not new when Lustig began composing printed matter from a common selection of type case material. However, Lustig's applications were more sculptural than most. His inspirations were the rule-breaking typographers who literally turned pieces

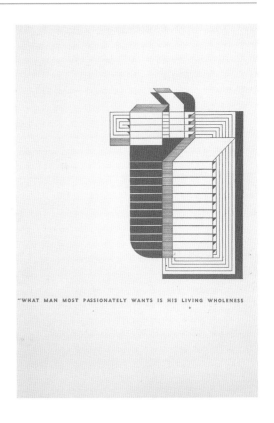

"WHAT MAN MOST PASSIONATELY WANTS IS HIS LIVING WHOLENESS

of lead upside down to make intaglio impressions. The upstart Dadaists used stock printers' "cuts" in their ad hoc compositions, and the revolutionary Russian Constructivists made the most of limited typographic availability by building letters and geometric ornament out of type case "furniture." This approach was adopted and propagated by artists working for various Eastern European avant-garde magazines, like *Blok* in Warsaw, *Ma* in Budapest, *Zenit* and *Red* in Prague, and *Tank* in Ljubljana. The Dutch typographer H. N. Werkman, who published a small typographic journal called *The Next Call*, made what he called "drucksels," which combined wood and metal letterforms with metal typesetting furniture.

Lustig did not have direct contact with these documents, but he certainly learned about them through the books and magazines he is known to have devoured.

A handful of printers in the United States were making typography with small proof presses in a traditional manner. Lustig nuanced his version to give a more contemporary look. He created compositions that included simple geometries—half-circles, squares, triangles—which looked a lot like children's stacking blocks. Once he was solidly proficient with his medium, the designs became increasingly complex—some curiously akin to intricate primitive tribal motifs or kaleidoscopic patterns, others similar to detailed architectural renderings. Despite the rigidity of this labor-intensive material, Lustig managed to produce results that were fluid and variegated. Ingeniously nonfigurative, they caught the eye but tweaked other senses as well. The more he created, the more this metal ornamentation became a personal signature—and a sought-after, marketable style. He never gave his assemblages a name, but he sold himself as a typographer/printer in brochures. Type case illuminations were what clients received from Lustig regardless of their messages.

BOOK MAN

Lustig's novel handiwork impressed the Los Angeles bookseller and literary impresario Jacob Zeitlin. Zeitlin's seemingly insignificant holiday card commission started a chain of events that ultimately established Lustig's reputation as a specialist in contemporary book cover design.

"In the Fall of 1937, Jake Zeitlin asked me to print his Christmas card from a design by a twenty-two-year-old lad who had come into his book shop seeking a design commission," wrote Ritchie about his first encounter. "Somewhere along the line he started creating colorful designs with geometrical printers' ornaments and rules. They were abstract and intriguing, and while printers had used 'printer's flowers' for centuries, arranging the pieces in decorative designs in lieu of illustrations, nothing comparable to Alvin Lustig's creations had ever been done. He created a new art form, virile, abstract and colorful."[25]

Opposite:
Christmas card, late 1930s.
Typographic experiment.

Top right:
Philately in Europe, 1939.
Catalog cover.

Bottom right:
Robinson's 58, late 1930s.
Cover, purpose unknown.

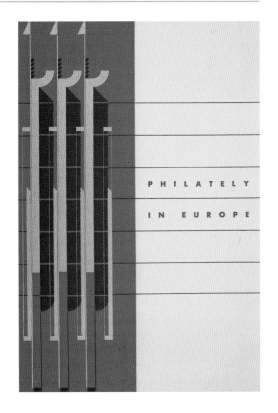

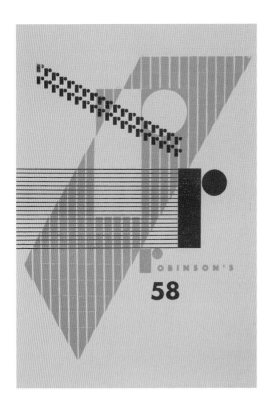

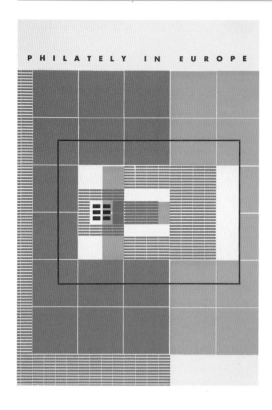

PHILATELY IN EUROPE

Above:

Philately in Europe, 1940.
Catalog cover.

Opposite:
Typographic experiment, late 1930s.
A progressive sequence of letterpress
impressions.

The first book entrusted to Lustig was William Van Wyck's *Robinson Jeffers*, a biographical essay about the storied American poet whose work focused on Central California. The text was short and "hardly substantial enough for a book," explained Ritchie in a 1983 letter. "I finally laid it out with the text taking up only two thirds of the pages and asked Alvin if he could create some designs to fill the rest. I remember it as a rather silly request—'make them flow as the movements of a symphony.'" What began as a means of padding out the text turned into a showcase for Lustig's unique gift. "The book was a tour de force in which the decorations overpowered the text, but it was fun," Ritchie concluded.[26]

Lustig subsequently designed a few jackets for Ritchie, including Gertrude Stein's *What Are Masterpieces and Why Are There So Few of Them?*, Aldous Huxley's *Words and Their Meanings*, and Herman Cherry's *Scrapbook of Art*, all with type case materials. But the project that "is as outstanding as any printed this century," touted Ritchie, was Alfred Young Fisher's epic poem, *Ghost in the Underblows*, edited by Lawrence Clark Powell.

To announce and pay for the book, Lustig designed an elaborate twelve-page prospectus containing testimonials and a "plea" for sponsors to contribute funds. The responses, including this from the poet William Everson, were triumphant: "You get the conception of an infinitely sensitive and intelligent man laying his ear to the earth and writing verbatim every delicate response and flux that twitches his being."[27] Offered to "subscribers," the book was planned in an edition of 275 copies at $6 each (it was assumed that the advance subscriptions would provide $1,650 for the production). Lustig's cover design was made entirely from type case slugs. Then Ritchie asked him to create an abstract typographic illustration for each of the ten books into which the poem was divided. "They were sensational, strong and vibrant in contrasting red and stark black. He also created an innovative title page spread across two leaves."

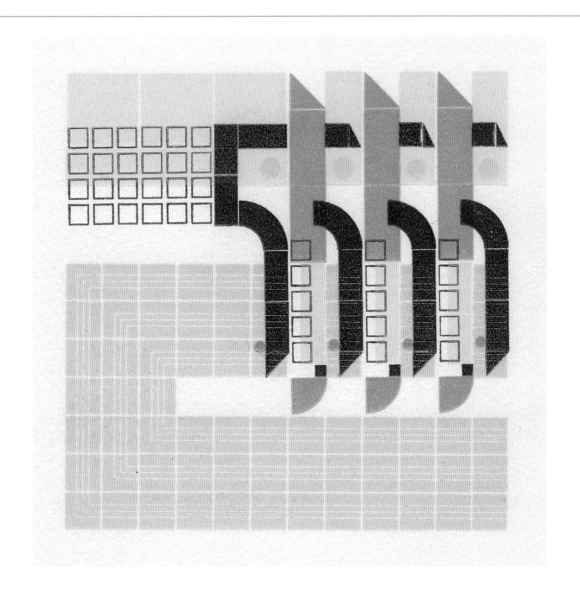

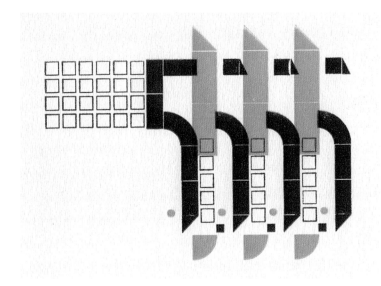

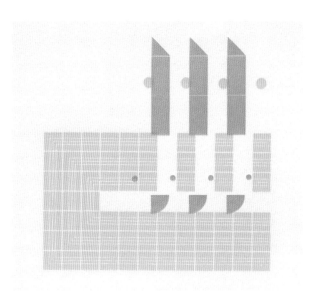

42

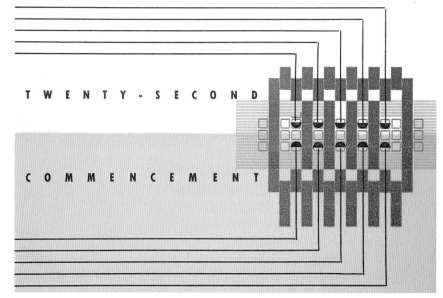

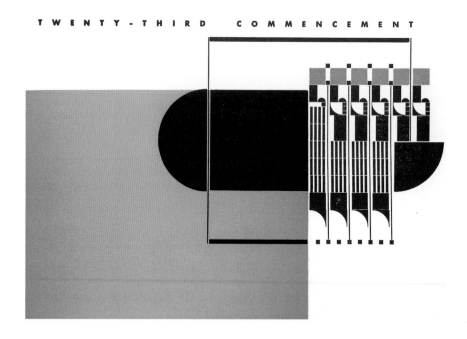

THE GHOST IN THE UNDERBLOWS

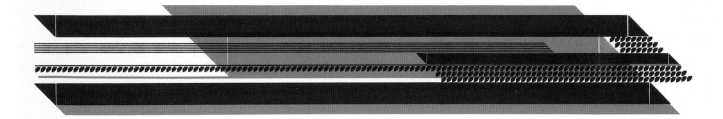

BY ALFRED YOUNG FISHER
EDITED WITH AN INTRODUCTION BY
LAWRENCE CLARK POWELL • DESIGNED BY
ALVIN LUSTIG AND PRINTED BY THE
WARD RITCHIE PRESS AT LOS ANGELES
CALIFORNIA • NINETEEN HUNDRED AND FORTY

Opposite:
Beverly Hills High School, 1939,
1940 and 1942.
Program covers for commencement
ceremony.

Above:
The Ghost in the Underblows, 1940.
Title page.

Following spread:
The Ghost in the Underblows, 1940.
Interior illustrations.
Lustig used geometric type case shapes
to create the abstract designs. The
process was arduous, but the results
were unique in American book design.

These "heroic type pictures," as Ritchie dubbed them, were nonetheless a "magnificent headache" and "bastard to print."[28] Lustig had collected the ornaments from various type sources, and they included some Monotype slugs and random bits and pieces from small-job printers, which meant that virtually every piece of metal was an awkward size. "While they were supposed to be accurate in picas, there was enough slight variation to make the forms unstable and loose elements were always popping out," explained Ritchie. When the second color was laid, it wouldn't always line up either. But Ritchie proudly noted, "Somehow we managed and the book eventually appeared without very many apparent imperfections." The book's design was as epic as the poem.

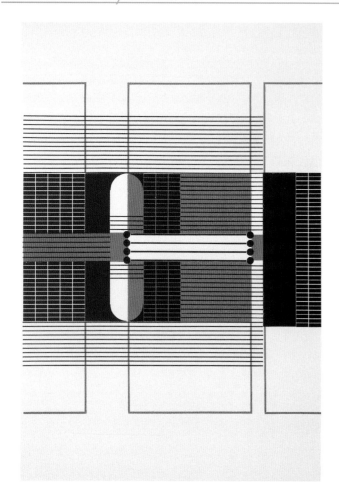

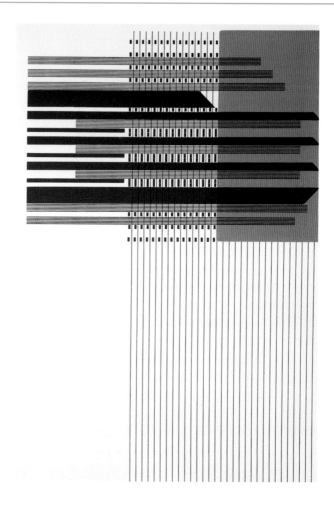

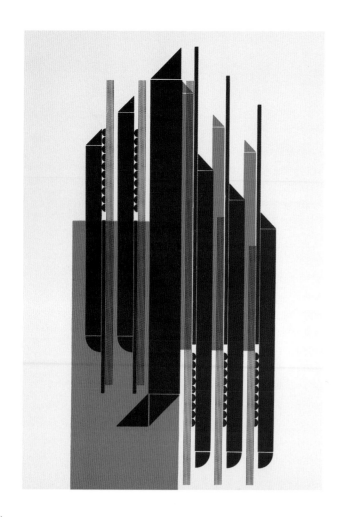

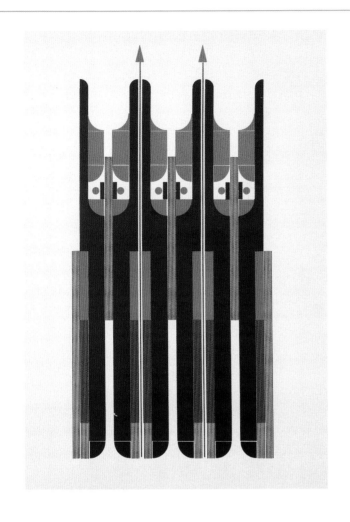
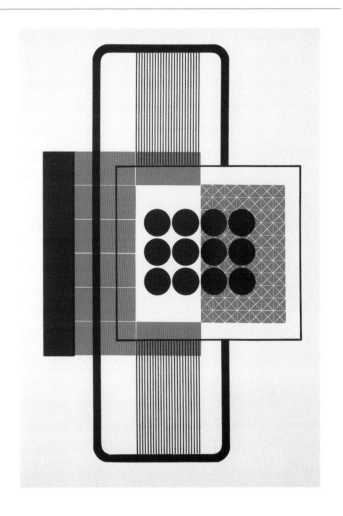

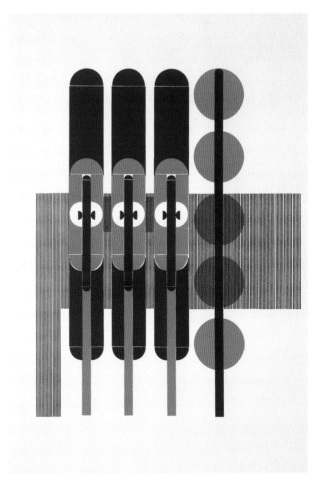

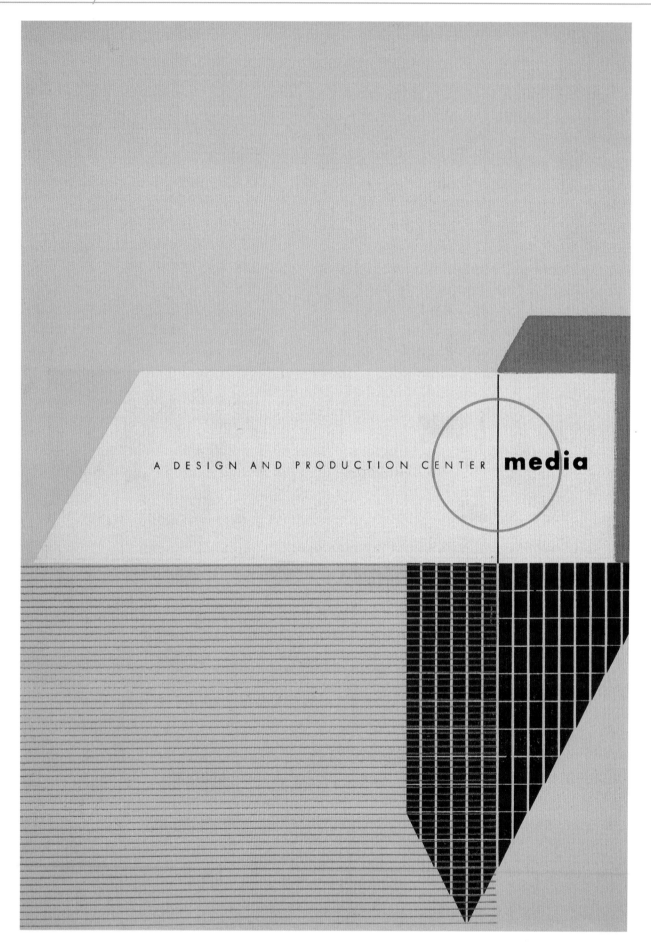

A DESIGN AND PRODUCTION CENTER **media**

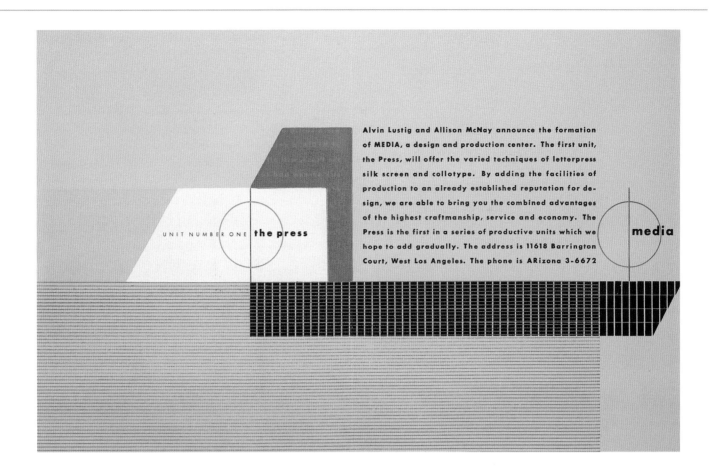

Alvin Lustig and Allison McNay announce the formation of MEDIA, a design and production center. The first unit, the Press, will offer the varied techniques of letterpress silk screen and collotype. By adding the facilities of production to an already established reputation for design, we are able to bring you the combined advantages of the highest craftmanship, service and economy. The Press is the first in a series of productive units which we hope to add gradually. The address is 11618 Barrington Court, West Los Angeles. The phone is ARizona 3-6672

UNIT NUMBER ONE the press

media

ENTER NEW DIRECTIONS

Ritchie remained one of Lustig's lifelong supporters, but another independent publisher and literary progressive emerged as an even more significant patron, friend, and confidant (judging from the hundreds of letters between them). Around 1940, Zeitlin introduced Lustig to James Laughlin, the audacious publisher of New Directions Books, founded in 1936, when Laughlin was only twenty-two years old. The imprint was devoted to Modernist writers, including William Carlos Williams, Delmore Schwartz, Ezra Pound, Tennessee Williams, and Henry Miller, which made it a somewhat risky venture. Like Ritchie, Laughlin was smitten by Lustig's type case designs. He commissioned Lustig to create a jacket for the 1941 edition of Henry Miller's *The Wisdom of the Heart*, (see pg. 49) a collection of short fiction and essays. Printed on a yellow background, the blue-gray decorative slugs, the bold red arrow, and the sans serif typography offer no clue whatsoever to the content of the book. Yet by virtue of this graphic enigma, the cover suggested Miller's avant-garde (and risqué) spirit—and

by extension, New Directions's own progressive character. Graphically, *The Wisdom of the Heart* "was quite unlike anything then in vogue," wrote Laughlin in *Print* magazine, "but it scarcely hinted at the extraordinary flowering which was to follow."[29]

Laughlin was obviously pleased but admitted that from his perspective the nonrepresentational construction, while suited to the book, was rather stiff. He nonetheless added, "A less fecund talent might have been content to work that vein for years, but not Lustig." While Lustig did apply the same approach to New Directions' next volume, *Selected Poems* by Carl Rakosi (1941) (see pg. 48), Laughlin was right—Lustig was on the verge of changing his method. In fact, Laughlin gave him the opportunity by quickly filling Lustig's dance card with jacket requests, including the first twenty-five volumes in

Opposite and above:

Media, A Design and Production Center, early 1940s.
Cover and inside for the announcement for Lustig's studio, The Media Press.

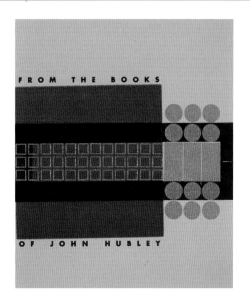

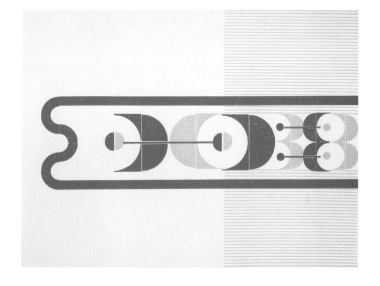

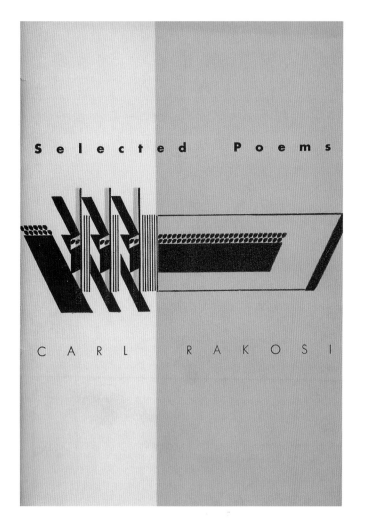

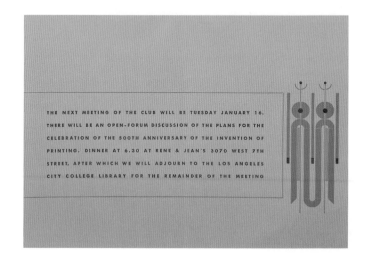

the New Classics reprint series of fiction and poetry. "Encouraged with a large volume of work," wrote David Davies in his unpublished manuscript, "Alvin broke away from his usual abstract designs and produced a wide variety of designs, all modern and all unlike any jackets produced previously."[30]

Lustig's series was indeed original. All the New Classic images were abstractions in two colors, some more representational than others, but always based on deep symbolic interpretations of the texts. For *The Longest Journey* by E. M. Forster (1943) (see pg. 53), an impressionistic maze vividly suggests the title; for *A Season in Hell* by Arthur Rimbaud (1945) (see pgs. 60–61), Arp-like shapes frame the distinctly surreal hand lettering; and for *Selected Poems* by D. H. Lawrence (see pg. 52), the suggestion of a phoenix rising from flames provokes wonderment over what the conceptual thread could be (even Laughlin professed some bewilderment).

"There was no need to 'design down' as there had been no 'writing down' in the books selected," Lustig wrote in a brief essay for a portfolio of jackets published in 1947 by the Gotham Bookmart in New York.[31] "Still it was necessary to attract and hold the roving eye of the potential buyer." He accomplished this by inventing symbols that quickly summarized the spirit of each volume. Sometimes the symbols were subjective, other times Lustig attempted to objectify and project the inherent concepts in visual form. He noted that obvious symbols were employed when necessary and "evasive" ones used when he wanted to capture an emotional quality. "It is obvious that the series of jacket designs which Alvin Lustig has made for my New Classics books is a constant pleasure to the eye," wrote Laughlin in the foreword for the same Gotham Bookmart portfolio. "There is nothing in the book world today which compares with them for color, for variety, for life, for appeal to the intelligence. Again and again I find myself lining the books up just to gloat over them."

Laughlin was not the only gloater. Lustig's jackets had a quantifiable impact on the book-buying public; they enormously increased the sales of the New Classics line. "About eight books

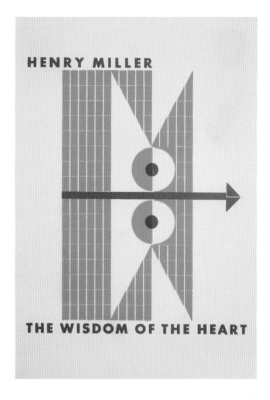

Opposite clockwise from top left:
John Hubley, early 1940s.
Bookplate for the United Productions of America animator.

Lucy Cady Van Buskirk Studio, late 1930s.
Annoucement of opening at the Stendahl Gallery.

Bohemian Life, 1940.
Envelope for the newsletter.

Rounce and Coffin Club, 1940.
Invitation for the 500th anniversary of the invention of printing.

Carl Rakosi Selected Poems, 1941.
Booklet printed at Lustig's Media Press in Brentwood for New Directions, Norfolk, Connecticut.

Above:
The Wisdom of the Heart, 1941.
Book cover for New Directions.

were in print before Lustig came into the picture," Laughlin noted. "They were jacketed in a very conservative, 'booky,' way. Sales were pretty dreary. Then we brightened the books up with the Lustig covers. Immediately, they began to move . . . It is perhaps not a very good thing that people should buy books by eye. In fact, it's a very bad thing. People should buy books for their literary merit. But since I have never published a book which I didn't consider a serious literary work—and never intend to—I have had no bad conscience about using Lustig to increase sales. His beautiful designs are helping to make a mass audience aware of high quality reading."[32]

Every time Laughlin opened an envelope from Lustig, he was surprised, he said, "because the range of fresh invention seemed to have no limits, I had supposed that his gift was a purely visual faculty. Or, watching him play with a pencil on a drawing pad, I thought that he had some special magic in his hands . . . The forms took shape in his mind, drawn from a reservoir seemingly as inexhaustible as that of a Klee or Picasso." Lustig seldom relied on literal solutions. His method was to read a manuscript to get the feel of the "author's creative drive," then restate it in his own graphic terms. This approach could easily be confused with art for art's sake, or style for style's sake, since the cover designs were so far from providing any literal clue to the plot or content. Lustig's jackets and covers demanded acceptance on their own merits as unique inventions. "Because each time, with each new book, there was a new creation," continued Laughlin. "The only repetitions were those imposed by the physical media."

The New Classic series book jackets
for New Directions 1944–1955.
These jackets marked a departure from
Lustig's type case composition. He was
influenced by Modern artists, such as
Paul Klee, Joan Miró, and Mark Rothko.

Top left:
A Room with a View, 1944.

Bottom left:
Three Tales, 1945.

Opposite:
Monday Night, 1946.

Clockwise from top left:

D. H. Lawrence, Selected Poems, 1946.

The Glass Menagerie, 1948.

Wilfred Owen, Poems, 1949.

Paterson, 1949.

Garcia Lorca, Selected Poems, 1954.

In the American Grain, 1944.

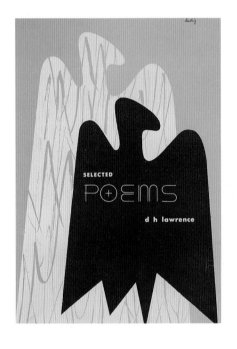

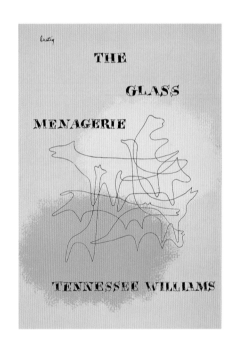

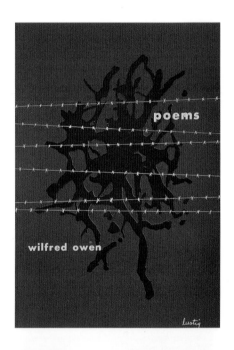

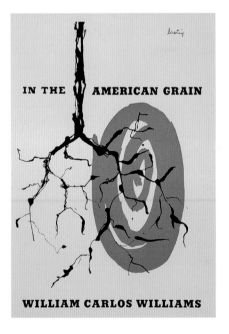

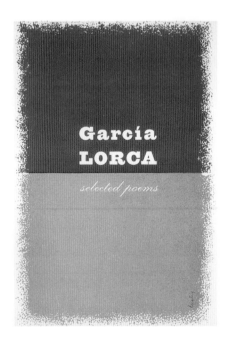

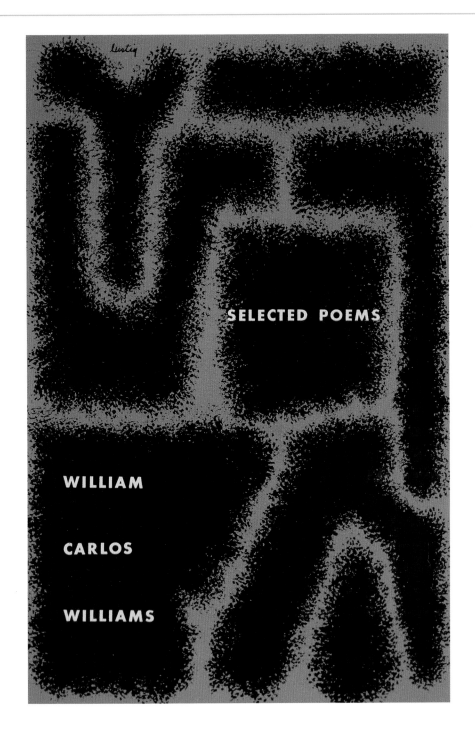

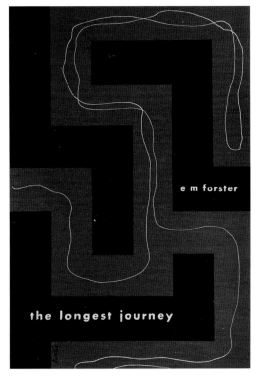

Clockwise from top left:
William Carlos Williams,
Selected Poems, 1947.

The Longest Journey, 1944.

Nausea, 1952.

THE DAY OF "THE LOCUST"

Nathanael West

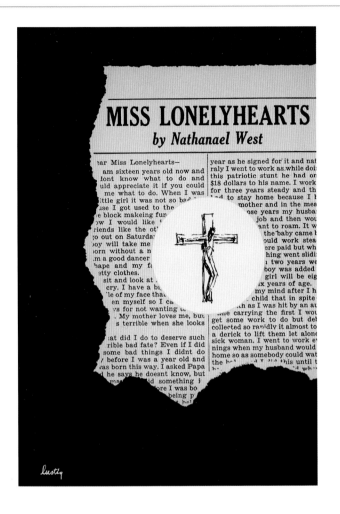

New Classics succeeded in the marketplace and also in the history of design for its ingenuity where other popular literary series, such as the Modern Library and Everyman's Library, failed, because of inconsistent art direction or dreary design. Each New Classics jacket had its own character, with visual unity brilliantly maintained through strict formal consistency. At no time did Lustig's look overpower, but it did establish an aura for the books. This kind of continuity was virtually unheard of in a publishing field where, according to Lustig's former client and friend Arthur A. Cohen, design is "wedded to rapidity and obsolescence, immediacy without subtlety."[33] Lustig's jacket designs for New Directions demanded contemplation; they were not just point-of-purchase visual stimulants.

Almost all the New Classics were hand drawn, including some but not all of the lettering. Yet Lustig was becoming interested in more mechanical techniques consistent with early modern European typo/foto experiments. In 1946, Laughlin was introduced to Lustig's next act of pictorial alchemy— extraordinary dark forms created by exposing raw film to different kinds of light in a darkroom. This prompted Laughlin to reflect, "Whatever the medium, he could make it do new things, make it extend itself under the prodding of his imagination. I often wish that Lustig had chosen to be a painter. It is sad to think that so many of his designs must live in hiding on the sides of books on shelves. I would like to have his beautiful Mallarme crystal [illustration] or his *Nightwood* abstraction on my living room wall. But he was compelled to

Opposite:
The Day of the Locust, 1949.

Above left:
Miss Lonelyhearts, 1946.

Above right:
The Wanderer, 1946.

work in the field he chose because he had had his great vision of a new realm of art, of a wider social role for art, which would bring it closer to each and every one of us, out of the museums into our homes and offices, closer to everything we use and see."[34] Although Lustig rejected painting as too "subjectivized," and never presumed to seriously paint or sculpt himself, he liberally borrowed from these arts and integrated them into his design.

The questions of what art is and who a real artist is came up often in letters Lustig exchanged with Laughlin (who Lustig referred to as "Jay"). In one such letter, concerning a possible article he asked Jay to write about him for the prestigious Swiss graphic design magazine *Graphis*, Lustig underscored that he wanted to be seen as a holistic designer:

> I appreciate all of the work you will put into the *Graphis* article. And if you don't mind I will make a few more suggestions as to the direction it might take . . . I am primarily interested in art for specific occasions—the more public the better. As you are well aware, public occasions of any significance or vitality are singularly lacking in our period, so that a person like myself is in a position of attempting to create not only the symbols, but the things they are supposed to signify. You know we have had a long-standing gag on my impending corruption because of the expanding scope of my work in relationship to 'worldly things.' I think you must be aware by now that a descent into hackdom and servility is as impossible for me as to retire into the world of personal vision occupied by the 'artist.' I think that it is in this effort to break down the barrier between art and life that the most challenging problem lies, and in which I feel my contribution might be made. To continue to 'invent' in the sense that the artist has done in the last fifty years is not as interesting to me as the problem of synthesizing and projecting these formal discoveries into a conscious reality shared on a broad level. In other words culture instead of 'art.' I think your article could certainly point out the pitfalls of such an aim as well as to judge my own capacities in relationship to it.[35]

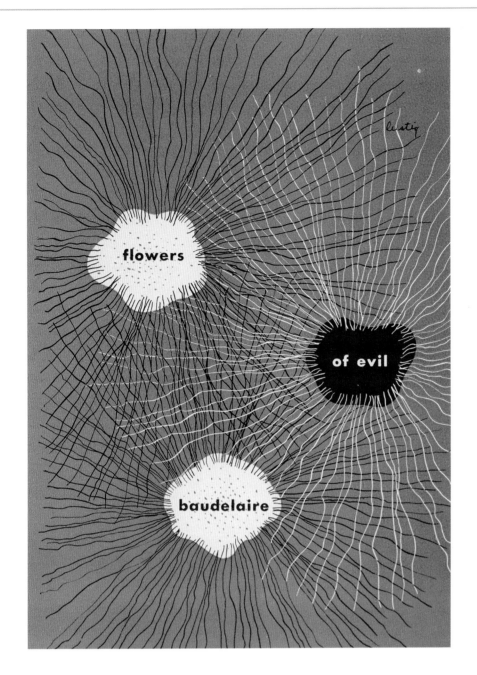

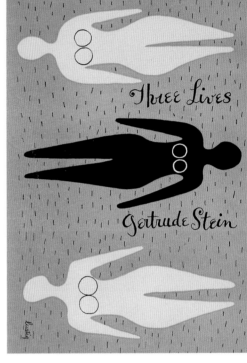

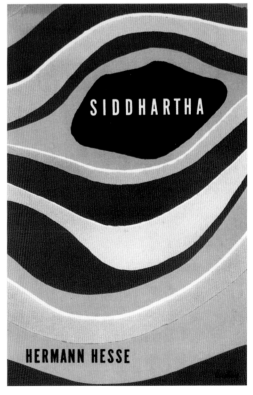

Opposite top:
A Handful of Dust, 1945.

Opposite bottom:
Amerika, 1945.

Above:
The Flowers of Evil, 1946.

Top right:
Three Lives, 1944.

Bottom right:
Siddhartha, 1951.

Clockwise from top left:
Under Western Eyes, 1951.

Mallarmé, Poems, 1950.

Illuminations, 1945.

Kenneth Patchen, **Selected Poems**, 1946.

ABC of Reading, 1951.

Ezra Pound, Selected Poems, 1949.
Art inspired by a desert plant
from Death Valley.

Opposite:
The Man Who Died, 1946.

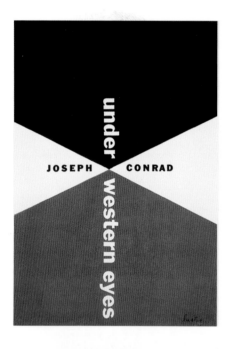

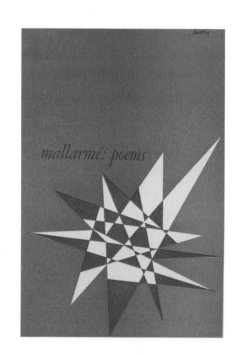

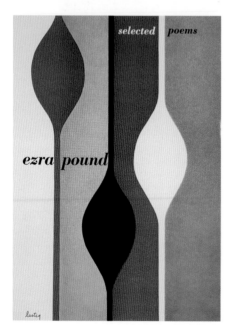

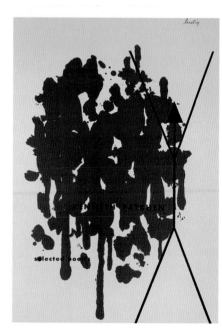

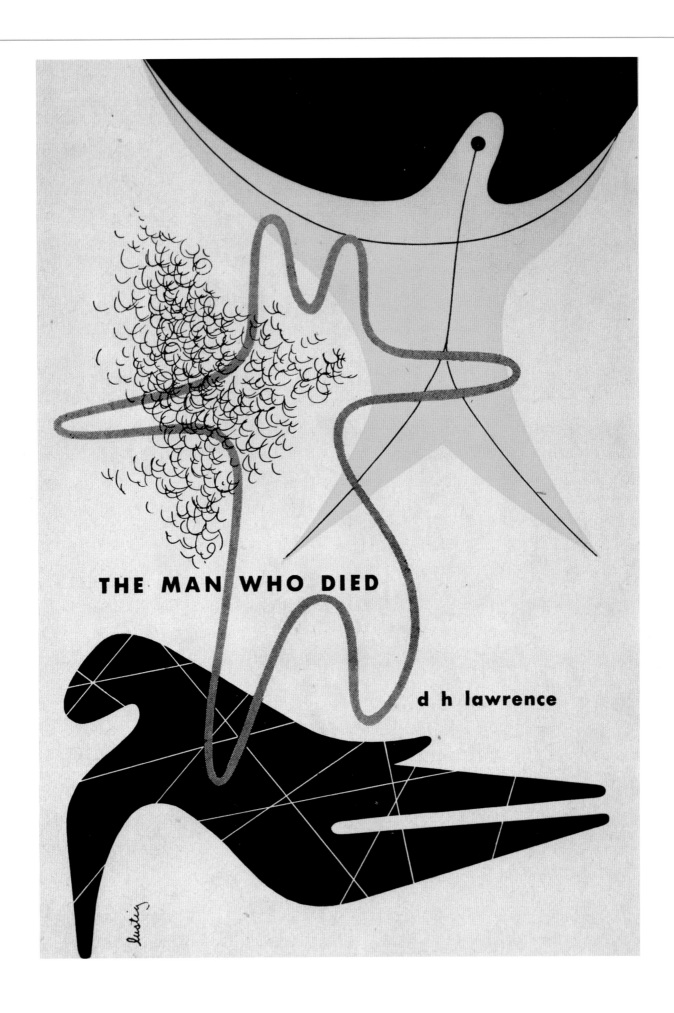

THE MAN WHO DIED

d h lawrence

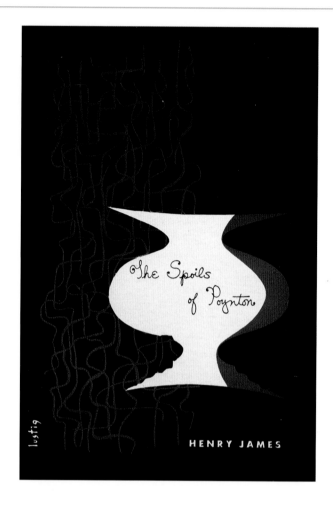

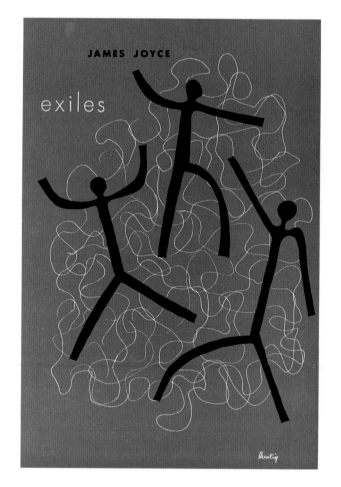

The *Graphis* article (which appeared in issue no. 23, 1948) was not ultimately written by Laughlin; nor did Lustig get his wish to be portrayed as a contributor to broader design culture. Instead, the English critic C. F. O. Clarke, though full of praise, focused entirely on Lustig's book work. "[They] were originally his private symbols, fruits of his own esoteric vision," he wrote. "The task, as he conceived it, was to find a series of symbols that could rapidly summarize the spirit of each book and give it an appropriate visual form." He pointed to the stark contrast of black-and-white figures superimposed on a dull red panel for Rimbaud's *A Season in Hell*, indicating "at once the plunge which the reader will make into the tense yet icy depths of the poem." While the red, white, and gold flames bursting in clear outline across the jacket of *Illuminations* (see pg. 58) "are again eloquent testimony to the emotional concentration of a poet whose work is nevertheless balanced by its intellectual discipline." And about Henry James's *The Spoils of Poynton*, Lustig captured the spirit and style of James, "The criss-cross of red threads endlessly intertwined epitomizes the way in which the author builds up his theme from the tireless annotation of psychological fragments."[36]

Lustig's design stressed the formal aspects of a problem, and he was precise to a fault. In an essay titled "Contemporary Book Design," he wrote: "The factors that produce quality are the same in the traditional and contemporary book. Wherein, then, lies difference? Perhaps the single most distinguishing factor in the approach of the contemporary designer is his willingness to let the problem act upon him freely and without preconceived notions of the forms it should take."[37] Lustig knew that the tradition of fine bookmaking was closely aligned with scholarship and humanism, and yet the primacy of the word, the key principle in classic book design, required reevaluation. "I think we are learning slowly how to come to terms with tradition without forsaking any of our own new basic principles," he wrote in "Personal Notes on Design." "As we become more mature we will learn to master the interplay between the past and the present and not be so self-conscious of our rejection or acceptance of tradition. We will not make

Opposite clockwise from top left:
The Great Gatsby, 1945.

The Spoils of Poynton, 1944.

Exiles, 1946.

A Season in Hell, 1944.

Above:
Reflections in a Golden Eye, 1948.

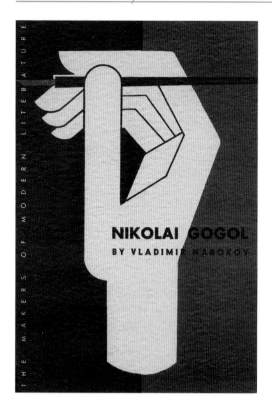

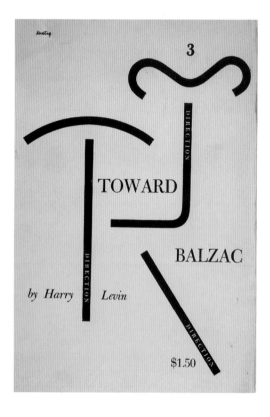

the mistake that both rigid modernists and conservatives make, of confusing the quality of form with the specific forms themselves."[38]

Although Lustig would probably have considered it but a small part of his overall output, no single project is more significant in the history of modern book covers, and possibly graphic design in general, than *Lorca: 3 Tragedies* (1948) (see pg. 72). It is a masterpiece of symbolic acuity, compositional strength, and impromptu lettering. Moreover, the late twentieth century preference among American book jacket designers for contiguous interrelated images, photo-illustration, expressionist typography, and rebus-like compositions can be traced directly to Lustig's black-and-white cover for *Lorca*. This grid of five symbolic photographs—the moon, sea, crucifix— each representing a tragedy, is bonded together by ad hoc lettering (Lorca's name was written and photographed in the sand) and linked through a curious, poetic disharmony. This and other distinctive, though today lesser known, covers for the New Directions Modern Reader series helped to transform a realistic medium—the photograph—into a tool for abstraction through the use of reticulated negatives, photograms, and still lifes. When Lustig began designing covers in the mid-1940s, covers and jackets were mostly painterly and illustrative, fashionably stylized, or ham-fistedly typographic. Hard-sell conventions, including literal renderings and large-title typography, were rigorously followed. It was here that Lustig entered taboo marketing territory, abstract imagery, and more nuanced typography.

In a letter to Laughlin, Lustig explained his rationale for the Modern Reader series as if the muse had just that moment struck him: "I have just come to the conclusion that I would like to do them all by photographic means. Using all kinds of methods, solarization, photograms, reticulation, negative melting, debossing, [and] montage I would create a set of vital images and symbols for each book. A certain number of drawn elements would also be used. Although much would be done with accidentals they would be combined in a very controlled manner that would have a shock effect. I see them

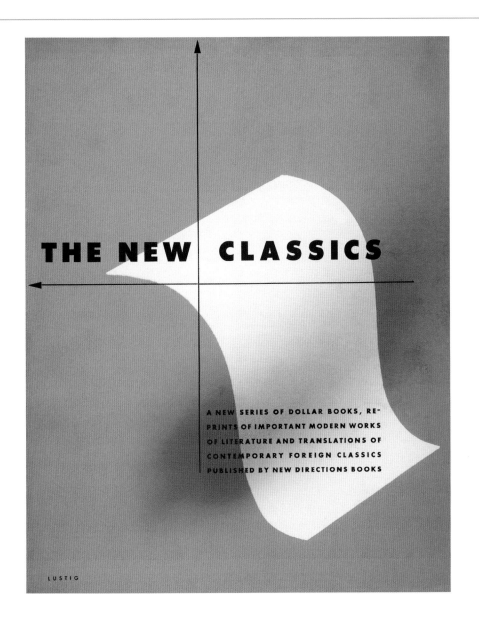

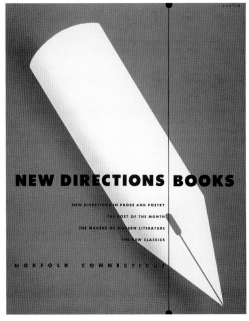

Opposite:

**The Makers of Modern Literature
and Direction Series**, 1940s.
Lustig made one design various
colors. The New Directions series
lasted throughout the decade.

This page:

The New Classics, New Directions,
and **The Makers of Modern Literature,**
c. 1940s.
Advertising point of purchase
displays, c. 1940s.

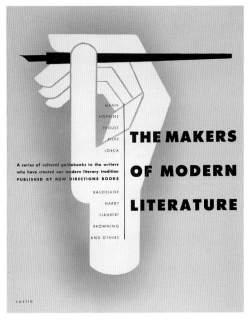

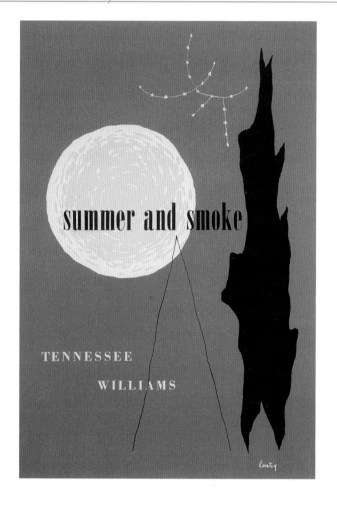

Clockwise from top left:
Summer and Smoke, 1948.

New World Primer, 1947.

Five Novels, 1949.

Opposite:
A Street Car Named Desire, 1947.
This was the original Lustig color; it
was reprinted later in red, but Lustig had
nothing to do with that selection.

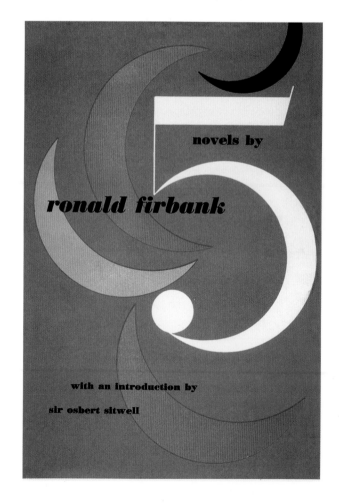

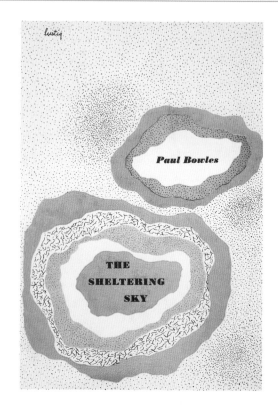

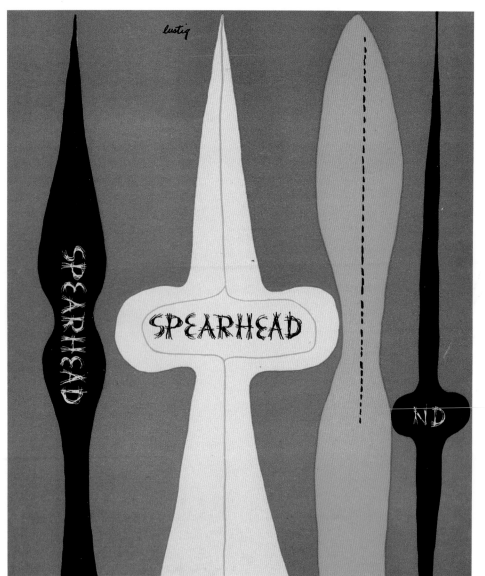

Clockwise from top left:
The Green Child, 1948.

The Sheltering Sky, 1948.

Spearhead, 1947.

Opposite clockwise from top left:
The Roman Spring of Mrs. Stone,
1949.

*ND 12, New Directions in Prose
and Poetry*, 1950.

*Dylan Thomas: Portrait of the
Artist as a Young Dog*, 1955.

Bread in the Wilderness, 1953.
Lustig did the complete book design.

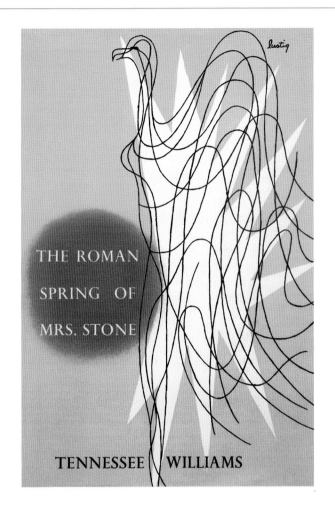

THE ROMAN SPRING OF MRS. STONE

TENNESSEE WILLIAMS

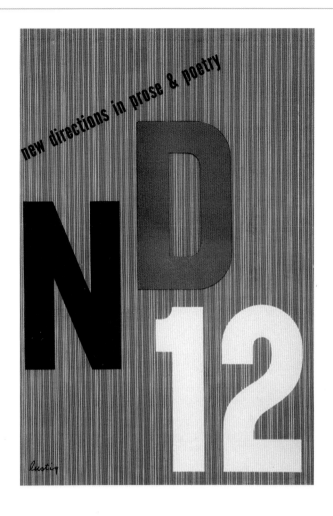

new directions in prose & poetry

ND 12

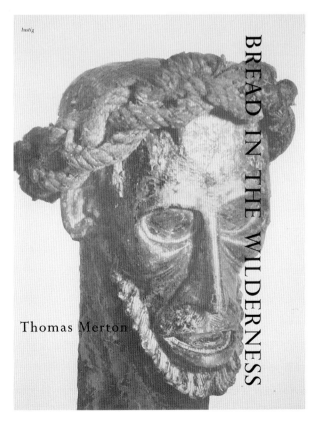

BREAD IN THE WILDERNESS

Thomas Merton

Dylan Thomas: portrait of the artist as a young dog

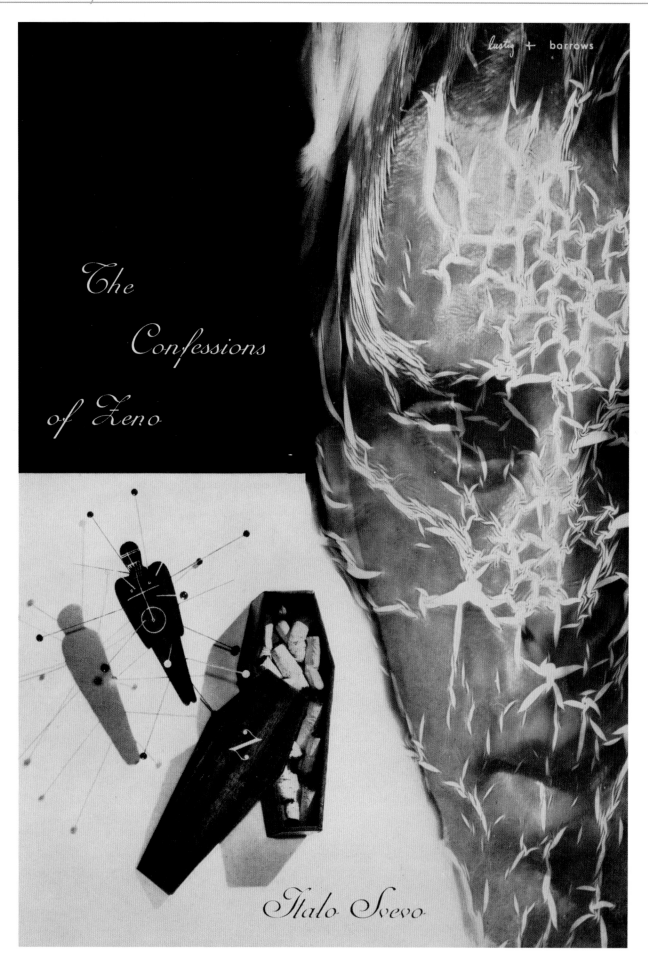

in two colors, perhaps one color remaining as a line cut. They would always be arranged as abstract forms against the background of the paper and would not be halftones covering the entire area. Nothing very good has been done in this field yet and this seems like a remarkable opportunity." He was right too. Although the European avant-garde designers like Alexander Rodchenko, Ladislav Sutnar, and László Moholy-Nagy worked with photography, few if any American designers did—although they would later.

Lustig ended his pitch with "the catch." Because there would be a slightly higher engraving cost owing to the halftones (which he avoided in the New Classic series), he asked for $150 rather than $100 per jacket. This added cost would cover photographic expenses and, when necessary, models. To further explain his process, he wrote a description of the cover for *The Confessions of Zeno* by Italo Svevo, arguably the most elaborate of the Modern Reader compositions: "I would like to photograph the back of a man's head and let it be the dominant form on the jacket. Interlocked within it would be for instance a few cigarette butts, symbols of the father, of the wife of the business partnership. Overprinting the whole thing in another color, would be some strange swirling forms to suggest madness. That sounds crude I know but it could be quite wonderful. The title of the book would also be integrated photographically into the symbols. Let me know what you think. I would do everything possible to avoid expensive engraving costs, by doing as much on my end as possible. This could be a real landmark in graphic design. There is a tendency in this direction, but no one has done a decisive job."

The Modern Reader series was further noteworthy for three reasons. Lustig set the series apart from all others by designing the covers to be printed in black and white (although

Opposite:

The Confessions of Zeno, 1946.
Photograph by George Barrows.

a few titles were, in fact, done with spot color). He worked hand-in-glove with photographers, who executed his vision for the first time (paying them $25 a photograph, and cosigning the work with them). And he created three-dimensional tableaux, a rare method in its day but extensively employed by a subsequent generation of designers. He also introduced the photomontage, which was a widely used Modernist tool but one that had been only occasionally used on book jackets. In the end he accomplished what he referred to as "a decisive job," or a convincing and alluring design.

The Modern Reader series was successful, and Laughlin gave Lustig considerable license to experiment with each jacket. Yet that did not prevent a measure of client interference. Letters between the two reveal some common creative tensions. In one dated January 2, 1951, Laughlin writes that he saw the premiere of Tennessee Williams's *The Rose Tattoo*, starring Maureen Stapleton, in Chicago. "I believe this play will be a considerable success in New York, and that we will sell a lot of books," he wrote. "I must tell you, however, that I have bad news for you about the hank of hair [included in Lustig's original comp for *The Rose Tattoo*]. I liked it very much, but Tennessee didn't like it at all." Laughlin half-jokingly added, "You must bear in mind that Tennessee does not have a very strongly developed visual imagination, and if things are not entirely sketched out for him it is hard for him to see them, and he becomes timid . . . I did not think it wise under the circumstances to press the point, and so I am saving the hank of hair for you and you can use it in some other jacket." Lustig, however, was sanguine about Williams's displeasure. In a response to Laughlin, he said, "don't worry about the Tennessee Williams business. It doesn't bother me a bit. Susan [Lustig's sister, who worked for Laughlin] called him a pudgy pill which about covers the situation." Of course, Laughlin was relieved, "I am awfully glad that you are not upset . . . I will keep the hank here, and you can pick it up when you come east. . . ."

In another exchange, Laughlin addressed Lustig's design for Joseph Conrad's *Under Western Eyes* (1951) (see pg. 58), which he describes as "one of the most fascinating books being

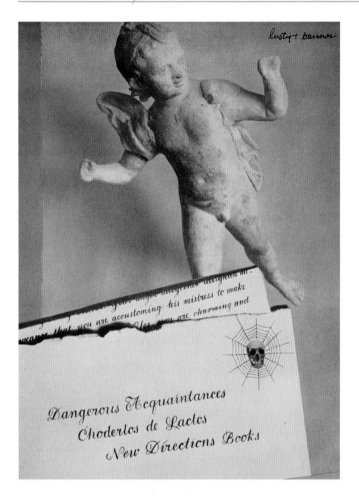

all about the Russians." The design, a rather uncharacteristically stark approach even for the New Classics series, is simply composed of the title set vertically in Franklin Gothic type dropped out of two arrow-like masses of color in white. "Thanks ever so much for your sketch on the Conrad jacket," Laughlin wrote. "I like it fairly well myself, but others here in the office are not a bit enthusiastic . . . And so I am wondering whether you would care to tinker around with it a little bit, and see if you can't develop it into something somewhat more lively. I like the general theme, but I would like to see it doing a little more visually."[39] This was not an isolated case, either. Responding to a sketch for a book of Ezra Pound's poetry, Laughlin wrote that people around his office were "not moved" by the "dull" color scheme. Lustig, who was usually accepting of such criticism, was rather exasperated and responded this way: "Now settle back we are going to have a nice long talk about the Pound design. When I sent it to you I felt that it was one of my finest designs, an attitude shared by my wife and staff. When the design was returned with the comment about 'dull' color, we tried many different combinations with lead in our hearts as none were as good as the original . . . I hate to sound smug, but when I think of the people on your office staff that you might have shown the design to compared to the people that have commented favorably at this end, I'm pretty sure that this end is a little heavier."[40]

On the whole, Laughlin was duly respectful of Lustig's choices. About the jacket for William Carlos Williams's *In the American Grain* (1944) (see pg. 52) he wrote that it "doesn't stir me profoundly, but you usually are right and perhaps I will like it after it is printed."[41] He usually saved his most stern interventions for times when design and marketing were at loggerheads, as they were with Herbert Read's *The Green Child* (1948) (see pg. 66). "I am troubled about the large expanse of white area," he wrote. "There is a terrible prejudice in the book stores against white jackets. They get dirty and then look badly on display."[42] The cover was, however, published as it was originally designed.

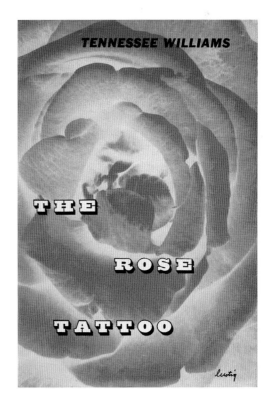

Opposite top left:
Dangerous Acquaintances, 1952.
Photograph by George Barrows.

Opposite top right:
Journey to the End of the Night,
1946. Photograph by Quigley.

This page, clockwise from top left:
Light in August, 1946.
Photograph by George Barrows.

27 Wagons Full of Cotton, 1949.

The Rose Tattoo, 1951.

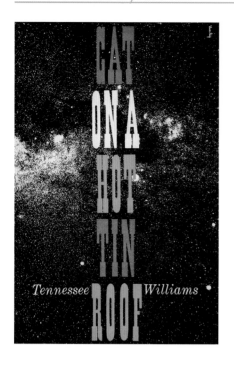

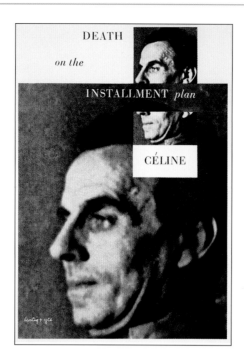

Page 72:

3 Tragedies, 1948.

Original hardcover (later paperback
was not revised by Lustig).
Photograph by J. Connor.

Page 73:

Camino Real, 1953.

Clockwise from left:

Cat on a Hot Tin Roof, 1955.

Death on the Installment Plan, 1947.
Photograph by Yee.

The Telegraph, 1953.
Photograph by J. Connor.

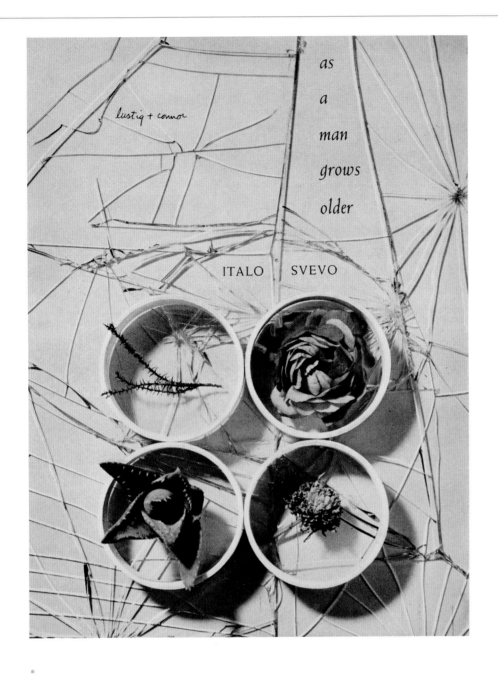

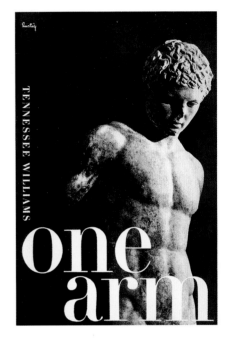

Clockwise from top left:

As a Man Grows Older, 1949.
Photograph by J. Connor.

One Arm, 1954.

Stories of Artists & Writers, 1953.

western advertising dec. '43

Payment was also a persistent issue. In one letter, Laughlin challenges Lustig's fee for designing the cover and interior of Thomas Merton's *Bread in the Wilderness* (1953) (see pg. 66), a book that was giving Lustig many production problems. "It seems to me that $350 is a bit high," Laughlin wrote. "We pay [another designer] $100 for design and supervision of production both. That is, for that amount, he gets all the estimates and buys the paper and cloth and all the rest of it. Of course, we have a little financial leeway because this title ought to sell, but still I don't think we ought to go much over $200 on it."[43] Lustig agreed to do it for $250. His relationship with New Directions continued until his death, at which time his wife, Elaine, designed some of the remaining covers.

THE FREELANCE LIFE

Lustig took on whatever additional graphic design his California clients had to offer. In 1940, he gave up his printing activities to devote himself solely to freelance design. In 1942, he began designing for the public relations firm Lee and Losh. "They are pleasant people to work for as they have no prejudices or pre-conceived ideas so give me almost unlimited freedom in my work," he wrote.[44] His first job for them was a brochure for the Aircraft War Production Council, a wartime

coordinating group composed of eight major aircraft manufacturers. Lustig also designed *Screen Actor*, the Screen Actors Guild magazine edited by his friend Molly Lewin, which was handled by Lee and Losh. He turned a drab members' journal into, as he put it, "something worth showing." Each cover of the magazine was an engaging collage of disparate but related symbols in the Modernist aesthetic. The logo also changed every issue. Another Lee and Losh project was a symbol for USO Camp Shows Inc., the organization that entertained American troops during World War II, which appeared nationally on all its trucks, posters, and film titles. And he was most excited about developing "a rather elaborate business called GRAPHICS," an extension of the graphical information firm The Pictograph Co. (the American arm of Otto Neurath's Isotype) to develop "methods of communication by graphic means at its most elaborate potential." As the war was ramping up, Lee and Losh's government connections were "apt to prove valuable," he wrote to Laughlin. Yet he ultimately declined the job as head of the Graphic Division of the Office of Facts and Figures, run by Archibald MacLeish as a U.S. propaganda office (the office also employed the Isotype proponent Rudolf Modley).

In 1942, Lustig was hired by John Entenza to redesign *California Arts & Architecture*, which was renamed *Arts & Architecture*. It was the first American architecture magazine to popularize the work of Richard Neutra, Craig Ellwood, Raphael Soriano, Gregory Ain, Pierre Koenig, Margaret De Patta, George Nakashima, Charles Eames, Frank Gehry, and many others who became Lustig's friends. It also featured articles by writers such as Esther McCoy, Edgar Kaufmann Jr., Walter Gropius, and Lewis Mumford. Lustig was ecstatic about the potential to do great things, as a letter to Laughlin reveals: "Have just been made art director of *California Arts & Architecture* with complete freedom as to form and with some possibility of suggestions editorially. This appointment will make possible my plan of just limiting my activities to a few accounts . . . Personally I believe it is one of the most potentially important magazines being published."[45] He was in total sympathy with the magazine's content and palpably

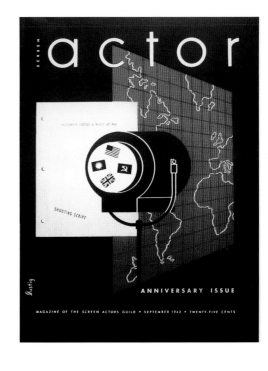

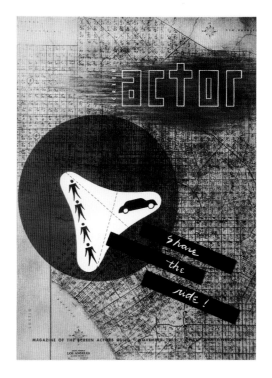

Opposite:

Western Advertising, December 1943.

Magazine cover.

Clockwise from top left:

Screen Actor, December, September,

and November 1942.

Magazine cover, for Screen Actors Guild.

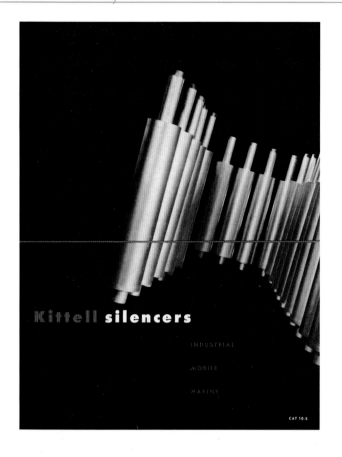

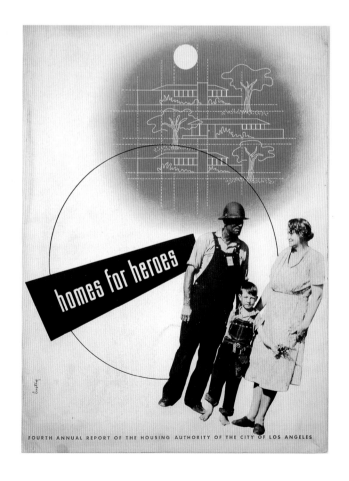

visual
communication
A YEARBOOK 1945

kill the "criticals"

AIRCRAFT LIQUID LEVEL GAGES

Roteron Instrument Company

SERIES 500 G

4800 MELROSE AVENUE, LOS ANGELES 27, CALIFORNIA

Clockwise from opposite top left:
Kittell Silencers, 1943.
Catalog cover for Kittell Muffler
& Manufacturing Co.

Kittell Silencers, 1943.
Inside page from catalog.

Homes for Heroes, c. 1944.
Annual report of the Housing
Authority of the city of Los Angeles.

Ski Alta, 1946.
Catalog for James Laughlin,
founder of Alta ski resort.

Clockwise from top left:
**Visual Communications,
A Yearbook**, 1945.
Unrealized book project
for *Look* magazine.

Kill the Criticals, 1943.
Catalog cover.

Liquid Level Gases, c. 1943.
Catalog cover for the Roteron
Instrument Co.

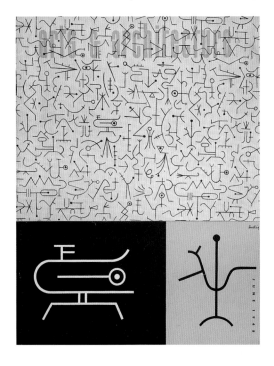

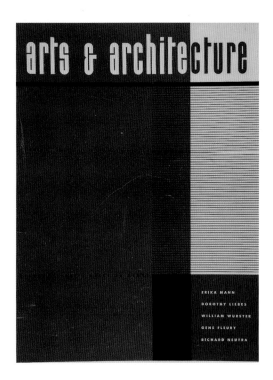

Top:

Arts & Architecture, June 1948.

Magazine cover.

Bottom:

Arts & Architecture, February 1942.

Magazine cover.

Oppsite:

Staff, March 28, 1944.

House organ magazine for *Look* magazine.

excited about the magazine "as it is becoming the perfect mouthpiece for my ideas." Lustig's covers for *Arts & Architecture* were stylistically similar to his book jackets and consistent with the magazine's Modernist tone.

Regrettably, this promising relationship soured within a year. Although Entenza professed respect for Lustig (and praised his work, Lustig said, in "daily letters"), an unhealthy rivalry ensued. Lustig believed the ill will was "entirely a matter of whether any other star can exist in the heavens, next to John Entenza." Adding, "it has taught me one thing however. To avoid once and for all those who make loud claims concerning their vision of the future and their dedication to it when all it hides is the shoddiest kind of vanity and selfishness."[46]

For a brief time in 1943, Lustig was director of graphics for *Western Advertising*, a trade magazine devoted to California ad agencies. His dramatic abstract cover (see pgs. 76–77) was a tour de force that took the Modern Reader method of photomontage to another level of visual intensity. And although he had commissions from Cannon Electric (for a booklet) and the Dana Jones Advertising Agency, as well as one-shots for the California State Bar Association, Los Angeles Housing Authority (*Homes for Heroes*, an annual report, 1943) (see pgs. 78–79), and the National Broadcasting Company, Lustig felt that significant work—work that would make an impact on the culture—was not all that plentiful in California.

NEW YORK BOUND

This lack of significant work was a good enough reason for Lustig to resettle in New York in 1944, when he was asked by Harlan Logan, editor and general manager of the behemoth mainstream magazine *Look*, to become the first visual research director of Cowles Publishing Co., the force behind *Look*. When John Lee of Lee and Losh got wind of the job offer, he wrote this to Logan: "Alvin [is] one of *the* best creative designers in the field of graphic arts in the country, and potentially, perhaps, the best. I was interested in graphics as one of the tools of public relations, and I hoped to help launch Alvin in a field wide enough to utilize his ability . . .

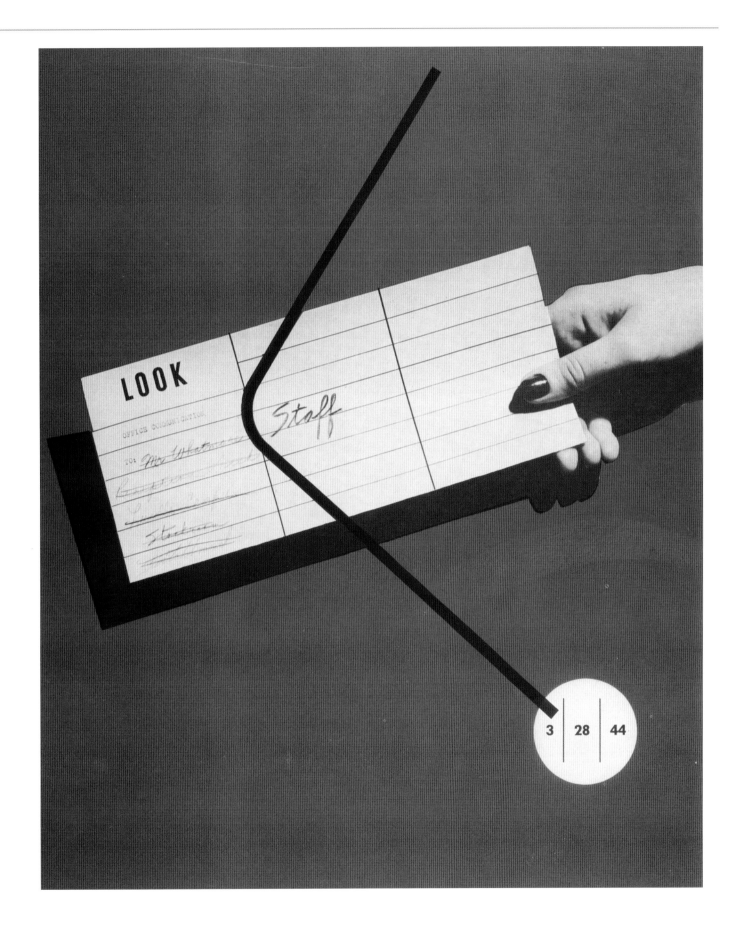

81

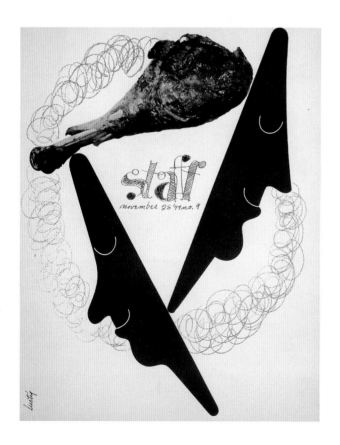

He has made quite a success of GRAPHICS, and could continue to develop his own operation. But I think he's ready for a wider field, and to reach the maximum of his capacity he needs the framework and the practical guidance of a large soundly-operated organization with a long-range program which can capitalize on original work . . . he could make a great contribution to *Look*'s development in the field of graphic design."[47]

Lustig was ready for the challenge. "Have succumbed to the lurid blandishments of the purple city," he wrote to Laughlin. "Start officially Feb 1. It sounds like a pretty wonderful job. Will be Logan's personal designer more or less, with some exciting projects on the agenda."[48] Lustig was given a brightly lit office and small staff, and the mandate to experiment using different graphic techniques and styles. *Look* wanted to develop a pocket-size magazine on the order of Esquire's *Coronet*, which never came to pass. But Lustig did design an avant-garde–spirited employee house organ—titled *Staff*—and promotional materials, including subway "car cards." True to habit, he also designed the interior of his office in a Lustigian Modern manner (see pgs. 126–128). The covers of *Staff*, like those of *Screen Actor*, gave him great scope. Since the magazines were not sold on newsstands, the logos were routinely altered, from comic hand lettering to minimalist modern type. The imagery, too, varied from Bauhausian photomontage (of a woman high diver floating in air) to a grid of image fragments similar to the one Lustig had used on the cover of *Lorca: 3 Tragedies*. He turned the entire project into something grand. With Logan's blessing, he began working on a book about visual communication and assigned Herbert Matter and Gyorgy Kepes to the project (the book was never published).

While at *Look*, Lustig was encouraged to build his freelance business. He produced all the advertising for the Hans Knoll agency (see pgs. 94–95) and covers and interior design for Reporter Publications, the publisher of *Men's Reporter*, *Gentry*, and *American Fabrics* magazines. The cover of *Men's Reporter*'s "Fun Number!" (1945) (see pg. 88), a colorful amalgam of Joan Miro-esque comically surreal forms, was similar to the French surrealist magazine *Minotaur*, but the

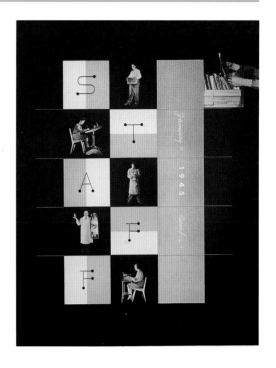

Opposite clockwise from top left:
Staff, June 18,1944; April 25,1944;
November 28, 1944; May 23, 1944.

Above:
Staff, June 9, 1945
House organ magazine for *Look*
magazine.

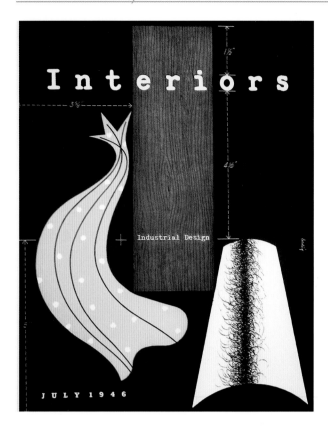

style had never previously been seen on any American retail magazine. Lustig also created covers for *Interiors* (July 1946) and *Fortune* (December 1946). The latter, shimmering with a graduated rainbow-colored background and a beautiful montage of jewels, is one of the most startling of mass-market magazine covers and one of Lustig's most sublime designs.

WESTWARD BOUND

The *Look* position abruptly ended with Logan's firing (the reason is not known)—and in an instant the valiant experiment was over. It didn't come a moment too soon, though. "Am pining away for California more bitterly everyday," Lustig wrote to Laughlin. "I figure that if I work hard and save money next year I can return with enough to get started on that little home in the west."[49] He returned to Los Angeles in 1946, and for the next five years ran an office specializing in architectural, furniture, and fabric design, while continuing his book and editorial work. To hire Lustig was to get more than a cosmetic makeover. He wanted to be totally involved

in an entire design program, from business card to office building. His designs for both print materials and office interiors for Lightolier, for example, are evidence of the total unity of his vision (see pg. 174). Yet even as his multidisciplinary design work was absorbing him more, print remained the bulk of his output.

Books remained very important to Lustig's livelihood. He designed *Skiing: East and West* with photographs by Helene Fischer (Hastings House, 1946) (see pg. 90) and *Native Arts of the Pacific Northwest* (Stanford University Press, 1949.) The Mergenthaler Linotype Company quoted him in an advertisement about selecting their Bodoni Book typeface for the latter, which won an American Institute of Graphic Arts (AIGA) 50 Books of the Year award. "Because Bodoni book relates extremely well to the most advanced ideas of design and typography, as well as to the more traditional concepts of form, it was well suited to the spirit and content of this book. Although the material displayed belongs to an older and different culture, the aim of the book was to show how closely related these forms were to our modern attitude." Lustig also did occasional work for E. P. Dutton; Watling & Co.; Farrar, Straus and Young; and the Museum of Modern Art (MoMA). For Behrman House, he designed the complete book for *Jewish Holiday Dances* (1949) (see pg. 90), a little gem in which he used layered photomontages, transforming a book about folk art into an exemplar of Modernism.

James Laughlin had introduced Lustig to Blanche Knopf, the wife of publisher Alfred Knopf, and the company's powerful president. Known for her close ties to European authors and as the editor of Sigmund Freud, André Gide, and Simone de Beauvoir, Blanche was no small name in the publishing world. So her interest in Lustig was extremely important.

Top left:
Interiors, July 1946.
Magazine cover.

Opposite:
Fortune, December 1946.
Magazine cover
(art director Will Burtin).

Fortune

DECEMBER 1946

lustig

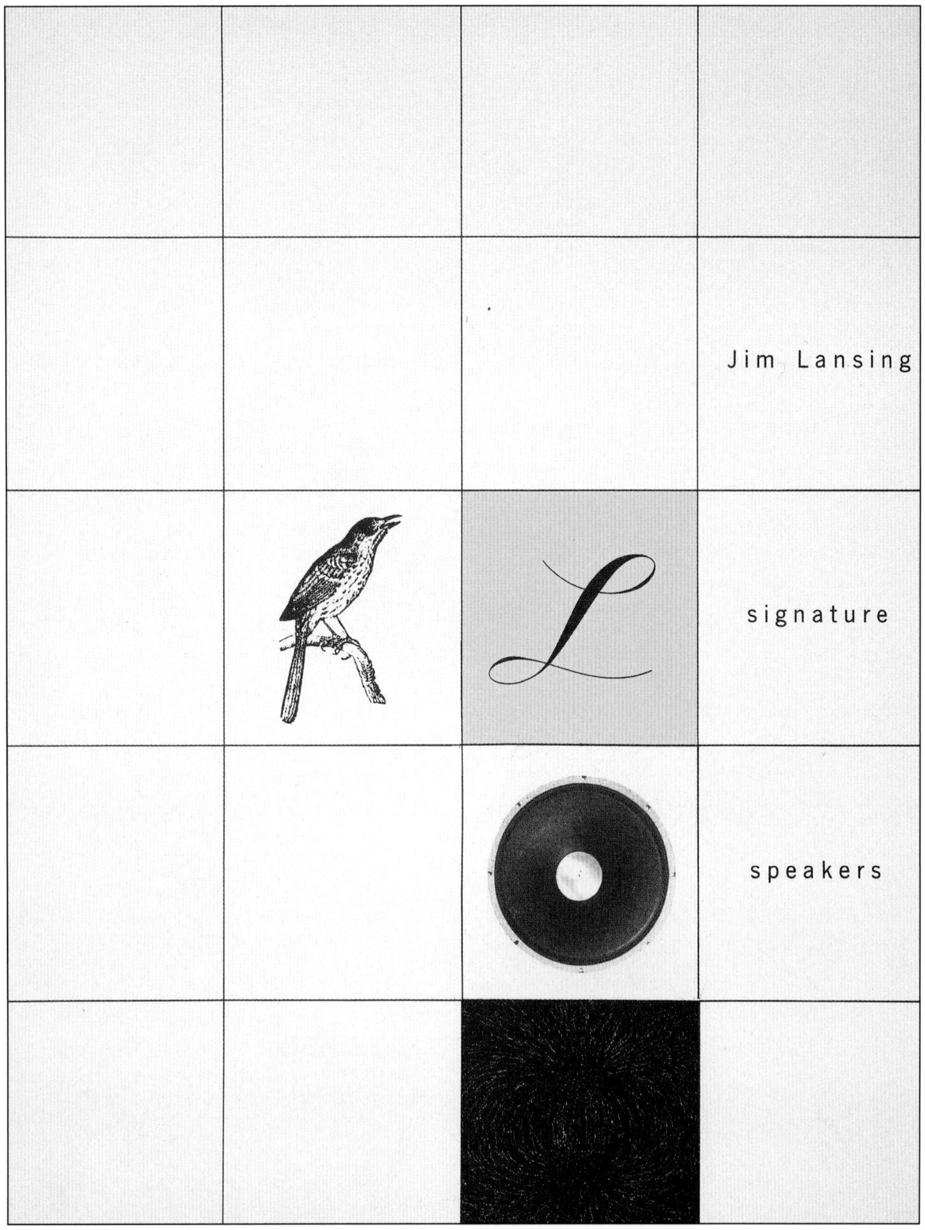

Jim Lansing

signature

speakers

This page:
Jim Lansing Signature
Speakers, 1949.
Catalog cover and inside spread.

Opposite:
Mister Magoo, UPA 1949.
Opening sequence for the animated
film. The visually challenged Magoo
walks out from the right and looks
through the eyeglasses.

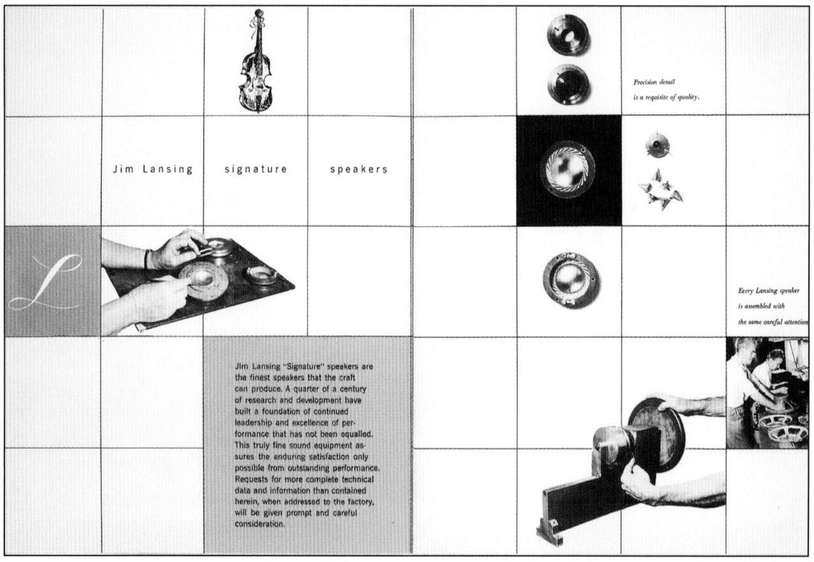

Jim Lansing   signature   speakers

Precision detail
is a requisite of quality.

Jim Lansing "Signature" speakers are
the finest speakers that the craft
can produce. A quarter of a century
of research and development have
built a foundation of continued
leadership and excellence of performance that has not been equalled.
This truly fine sound equipment as-
sures the enduring satisfaction only
possible from outstanding performance.
Requests for more complete technical
data and information than contained
herein, when addressed to the factory,
will be given prompt and careful
consideration.

Every Lansing speaker
is assembled with
the same careful attention

She commissioned him to work on more than a dozen books, including some very important titles. "My stock is very high at Knopf's at the moment . . . I find it necessary to have a modest bodyguard in order to keep off admiring authors, clamoring for my jackets," Lustig facetiously wrote. "It's all in the touch."[50] His jacket for *Monsieur Teste* by Paul Valéry (1947) (see pg. 90) featured one of his nervous line drawings set against a flat color background and also embossed on the binding. (The book was awarded an AIGA 50 Books of the Year award that year.) Nonetheless the one-off jackets for Knopf were not as uniform (or inspired) as the New Directions covers had been.

Lustig's star continued to rise in Los Angeles. In 1947, he began working with architect Sam Reisbord, with whom he designed the Beverly Carlton Hotel (see pgs. 145–147) and the Beverly Landau apartment complex (see pg. 149). He started teaching at Art Center—the first of a string of innovative design classes and programs he would initiate. And that same year he met Elaine Firstenberg, an art student,

whom he married in 1948. She helped with paperwork and bookkeeping in his design office but was not allowed to do any design work. Nonetheless, she picked up Lustig's design principles through a kind of osmosis, and after his death, she assumed his current jobs and picked up new clients for the studio.

AD MAN

Although not as prominent as Paul Rand in the advertising universe, Lustig was an inventive advertising designer. He was not an ad man in the strict or even liberal sense. He never designed the kinds of mass-market campaigns that Rand did. But he gathered an impressive client roster, mostly in the furniture and interiors industries—clients who understood that being modern was essential to piquing the interests of their customers. Lustig had the ideal aesthetic sensibility for this purpose. For clients like Knoll, Paramount Furniture, Menasco Manufacturing Company, Lansing Sound, Laverne Fabrics, and Miller Lighting Co. he created elegantly minimalist ads. In a departure from his usual design-related

Above:

Men's Reporter, November 1945.

Magazine cover.

Opposite:

Anatomy for Interior Designers, 1946.

Book jacket

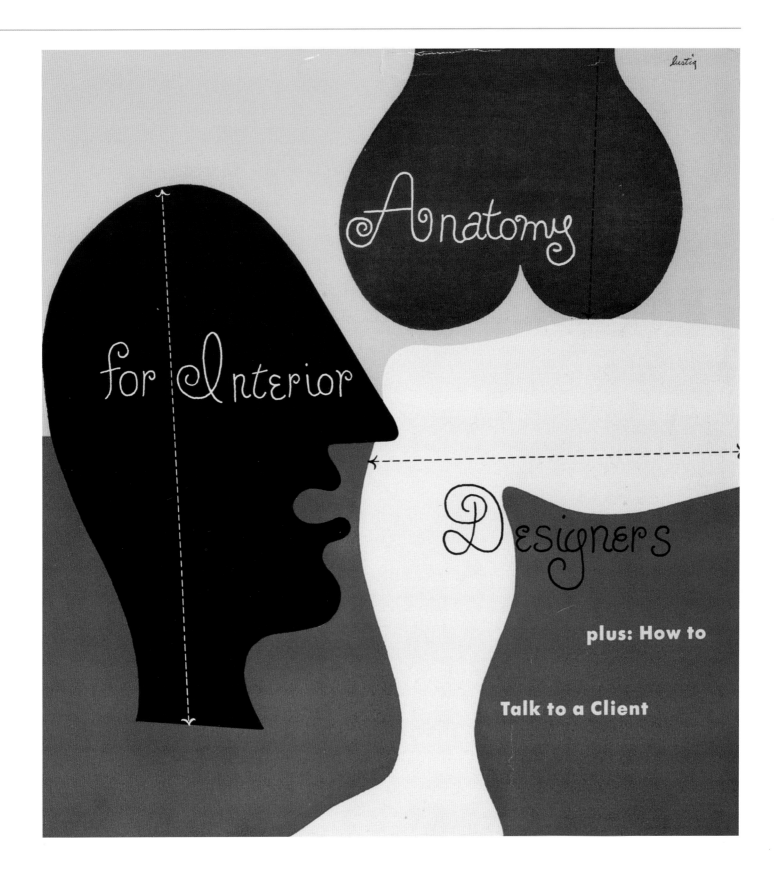

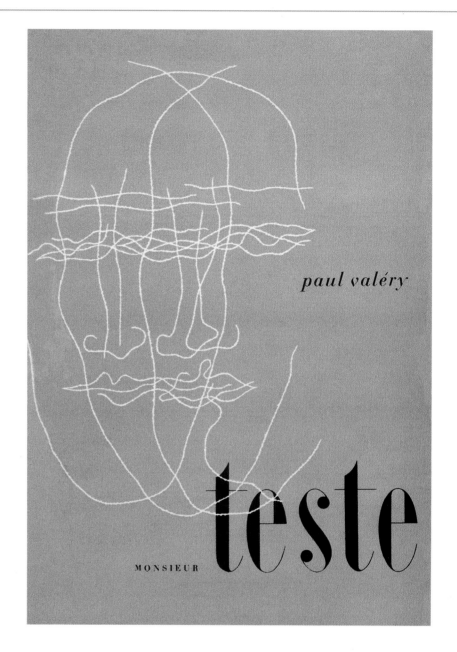

Clockwise from top left:
Jewish Holiday Dances, 1947.
Book design and inside page.

Monsieur Teste, 1947.
Book design and book jacket.

Skiing East and West, 1946.
Book design and book jacket.

Opposite top row from left:
Dark Green Bright Red, 1950.
Book jacket.

Parenthesis, 1945.
Book jacket.

F de N S, 1953.
Book design and book cover.

Opposite middle row from left:
AIGA Journal, Vol. IV No. 1–2, 1952.
Journal cover.

American Fabrics, 1951.
Magazine cover.

Industrial Designer in America, 1954.
Book jacket.

Opposite bottom row from left:
The Outsider, 1950.
Book jacket.

Two Legends: Oedipus Theseus, 1950.
Book jacket.

The Final hours, 1953.
Book jacket.

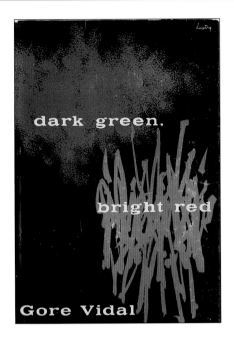

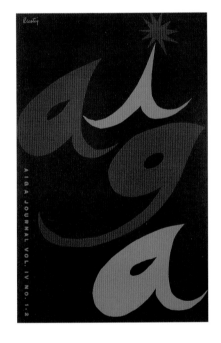

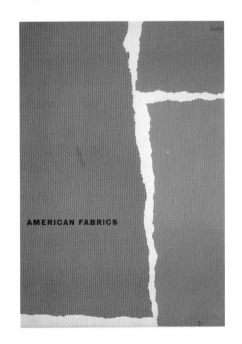

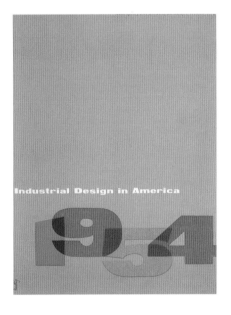

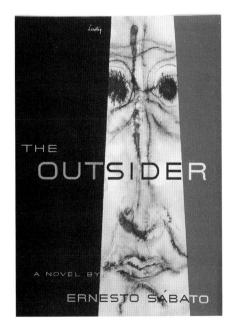

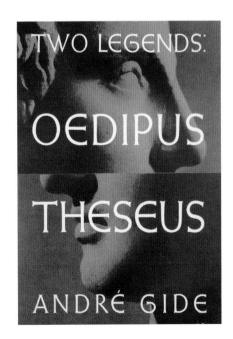

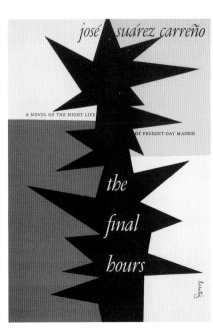

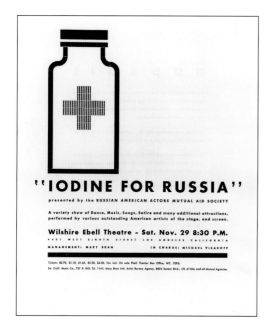

●

Top:

New Directions, 1945.

Advertisement in *View* magazine.

Bottom:

Iodine for Russia, 1943.

Advertisement for the Russian
American Actors Aid Society.

●

Opposite:

Power in Motion, 1942.

Advertisement for Menasco power
and hydraulics company.

clientele, he also developed a lighthearted ad in 1945 for
Jayson shirt company. At the same time, he designed various New Directions seasonal book announcements. Curiously, he cared as much for these ads as for any of his more
creative work; always a perfectionist, he applied the same
principles—clarity, economy, and acuity—when designing
the printed page, whatever the purpose. Creating advertisements may have required a slightly different mindset but
demanded the same refined compositional flair.

Every Lustig advertisement is consistent with the abstract
mannerisms in his book and magazine work. For instance, his
1951 ad for the Container Corporation of America (see pg. 99)
reflects growing interest in nineteenth-century wood types,
which he later used on Meridian book covers. Viewed as an
oeuvre, these ads further define the soft-sell, experimental
stage of American advertising, just prior to the full-scale
blast in the mid-'50s of the Big Idea "Creative Revolution,"
the progressive approach that introduced "creative teams"
of writer and art director, throughout mainstream media.

Lustig's ads are reminiscent of those designed by Paul Rand,
Lester Beall, Leo Lionni, Alexey Brodovitch, and Erik
Nitsche, but they are not imitations. They were often more
spare or playful in a painterly way. Lustig was not very fond
of Rand's El Producto cigar ads, which he found too coarse,
but he did admire Beall's collages.

All of Lustig's jobs were interrelated. An example from his
increasing practice in interior design illustrates this fact. In
the late 1940s, Lustig contracted with Paramount Furniture,
a custom chair manufacturer, to make him some chairs. They
took a keen interest in his work and agreed to produce a new
comfortable chair to rival the recently released Saarinen womb
chair, which was very expensive. Lustig had addressed the
problem of the high manufacturing cost of the Saarinen chair
and reasoned that an upholstered, plywood, molded chair in
two parts rather than one would solve the problem, and that
the chair could be sold at half the price. Once his chair was in
production, Lustig insisted on designing the advertisement
for trade magazines. Similarly, while working on another

power in motion

Transforms the forces of War

into the implements of Peace.

menasco

Manufacturing Company

Power-Hydraulics

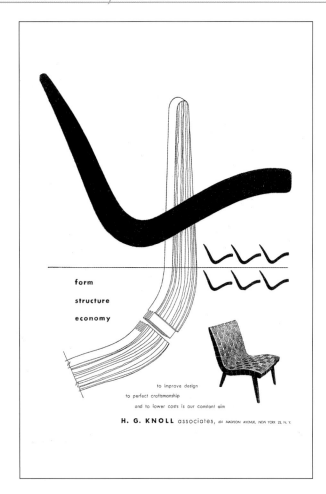

form
structure
economy

to improve design
to perfect craftsmanship
and to lower costs is our constant aim

H. G. KNOLL associates, 601 MADISON AVENUE, NEW YORK 22, N. Y.

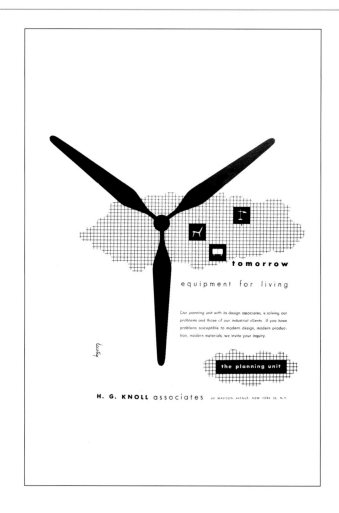

tomorrow

equipment for living

Our planning unit with its design associates, is solving our
problems and those of our industrial clients. If you have
problems susceptible to modern design, modern production, modern materials, we invite your inquiry.

the planning unit

H. G. KNOLL associates   601 MADISON AVENUE, NEW YORK 22, N.Y.

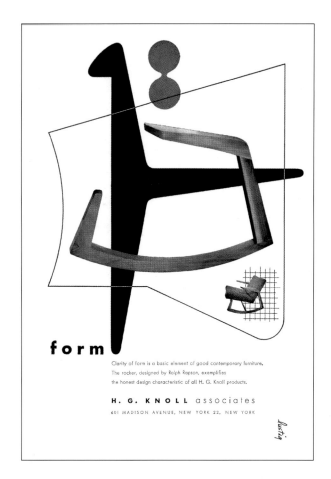

form

Clarity of form is a basic element of good contemporary furniture.
The rocker, designed by Ralph Rapson, exemplifies
the honest design characteristic of all H. G. Knoll products.

H. G. KNOLL associates
601 MADISON AVENUE, NEW YORK 22, NEW YORK

form
structure
economy

this mark of the three plus signs . . . symbols of
clean design, sound construction and low cost
will from now on help you to identify our products:
furniture . . . equipment for living . . . developed
by our Planning Unit. Send your name for our new
catalog to 601 Madison Avenue, New York 22, N. Y.

H. G. KNOLL *associates*

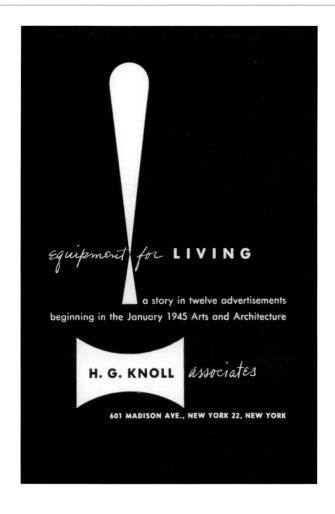

interior design project, Lustig met the Lavernes, owners of
Laverne Co. in New York, who produced a line of fabrics.
They, in turn, commissioned him to design a fabric titled
"Incantation," based on the witty glyphs on his New Directions book jackets. Of course, Lustig insisted on designing
the advertisement for his own product (see pg. 96). He hated
Laverne's horsey logo but cleverly managed to work it into
a handmade three-dimensional structure in his ad.

In contrast to agency practice, which required intensive
hard-sell presentations, Lustig rarely made formal pitches to
clients. Neither did he go out looking for ad work. Instead,
clients came to him. He would completely redesign the client's
"attitude" about a project, and clients were attracted to this
charisma. Clients came to him because they liked something
that he had done, or, more often, by recommendation of architects, art critics, and museum curators. The famed architect
Philip Johnson, one of Lustig's ardent supporters, introduced
him to the owners of Miller Lighting Co., which resulted in
Lustig designing a small-space typographic ad campaign for
them (one of the few he did not sign).

Man's constellation
finds many forms
and printing manifests it

Alvin Lustig

PRINTING: THE ART PRESERVATIVE OF ALL THE ARTS

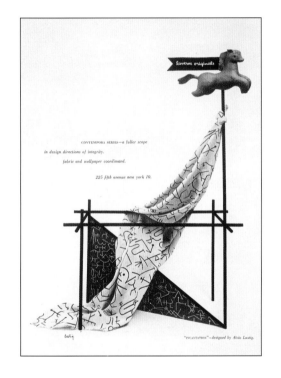

laverne originals

CONTEMPORA SERIES—a fuller scope
in design directions of integrity.
fabric and wallpaper coordinated.

225 fifth avenue new york 10.

lusty

"INCANTATION"—designed by Alvin Lustig.

"I WANT A THIN GOTHIC..."

While some of our customers specify type in this way,
most of them are meticulous about designating
face, size, foundry and pedigree.
We're fond of both kinds.
As conscientious fellows we'll track down
the type of your desire with only the vaguest description
of its peculiarities. Our people are trained for just
this kind of sleuthing, so call us when you have a type problem,
or even when you haven't.

THE COMPOSING ROOM, INC.

130 West 46th Street, New York 36, New York

JUdson 2-0100

A REQUEST ON YOUR LETTERHEAD WILL BRING YOU OUR NEWS GOTHIC SPECIMEN FOLDER

Although designing advertisements did not generate enough income to be more than a sideline, the advertisements advanced Lustig's graphic ideas. The 1942 ad for Menasco (see pg. 92), manufacturers of power and hydraulic machines, for example, prefigured Lustig's most innovative montages for New Directions books, while the more typographically subdued ad for *Screen Actor* magazine echoed the minimalist type play of later Noonday and Meridian book covers, which came about in the early 1950s.

Lustig's earlier ads were decidedly more surreal and conceptual than subsequent ones. That the later work is cooler may be attributed to his declining vision, which started deteriorating when he was thirty-eight. By age thirty-nine, he could distinguish only lights and darks. One of Lustig's great strengths was his finely honed ability to visualize the problem before him in both two and three dimensions, and this made it possible for him to continue designing despite his blindness. Even at the end of his life, he was actively designing everything he could, including advertisements, by dictating what he pictured in his mind's eye to his assistants, who transformed his words into concrete form. This keen ability to conjure the perfect color, type, and image continues to make Lustig's short life's work compelling. His advertising work is an important piece of his creative development.

MARKED MAN

Lustig was a prodigious designer of trademarks and letterheads for Southern California firms. Although he was not necessarily thought of as a logo designer like Lester Beall or Paul Rand, his marks underscored the aesthetics of his times. His most elegant was for Monte Factor (1947), a men's clothing store in Beverly Hills—a semiabstract outline of a cavalier in cape and with sword, tagged with a Bodoni "F" dropped out of a black square (see pg. 142). In *Seven Designers Look at Trademark Design*, Lustig explained his formal considerations: "The quality most desirable in a trademark, other than its power to identify and communicate, is its ability to resist change. The American trademark suffers to a considerable degree from being dated, and there are few marks of large

Clockwise from opposite top:
Ninth Graphic Arts Production Yearbook, 1950.
Double-page spread.

I Want A Thin Gothic, 1949.
Advertisement for
The Composing Room,
New York.

Laverne Originals, 1948.
Advertisement for "Incantation"
fabric by Lustig.

Above:
World Inventors Exhibition, 1947.
Brochure.

companies that do not seem distressingly old fashioned."[51] He asserted that quick dating usually comes from confusion of "formal" ideas rather than "content" ideas and that "the client in seeking for a mark that will describe a product or process usually thinks in terms of a small and simplified illustration rather than a mark as such."

While illustration is "susceptible to overtones of fashion and fad," Lustig thought that with the right touch, an illustration could be effective. The Monte Factor mark grew out of the needs to show sartorial elegance and to reduce a complex figure to a simple form, which would work in every size from a small label to a large point-of-purchase display. By selecting a historical figure and gradually reducing it to a diagrammatic form, Lustig reached a final mark that does the job. It required seventy-five drawings to reach this form. "Simplicity," Lustig wrote, "would seem to be a desirable quality, but in itself is no guarantee of universality." But he added that "freely drawn, orthographic forms can be just as lasting in character."[52] In Lustig's view, other elements are well suited for use in logos. Initials, like the swirling monogram he designed for the film star Alan Ladd (1949) (see pg. 103) was an abstract double entendre. The logo for a fancy barbershop called Comb & Shears (1949) (see pg. 103) was a linear drawing of comb and shears that was modern (sleek) with old-fashioned undertones (literal).

Lustig had a keen sense of how to make "old fashioned" elements look contemporary, but he also knew how to create marks from whole cloth (or type). His first logo design for UPA (United Productions of America) in 1946 (see pg. 104) was a textbook example of modern form based on memorable lettering. The curvilinear letterforms with dots as endpoints evoked modern furniture and gave the company a progressive aura. Nonetheless, he revisited the logo in 1950 (see pg. 104), changing it to three ellipses, each containing one of the letters U, P, and A. "The UPA," wrote Lustig, "is a very lively and talented group of men in Hollywood who are producing probably the finest animated cartoons in America today . . . The first [logo] produced a few years ago was perhaps a bit more elegant and worked well on stationery,

but did not satisfy the requirements for film." Since it was monotone, it failed to give the necessary impact. "As color is an integral part of their work, it was planned to emphasize it more than usual, event [*sic*] to the point of using four colors on all the stationery."[53] Lustig rejected the trite symbols of film and determined that a discreet signature would be more effective—and joyful. (Incidentally, in 1952 Lustig designed the opening sequence for the popular animated cartoon series Mr. Magoo; see pg. 87.) Most of his marks for others were similarly invested with a playful quality. Predictably, the letterheads for his own studio were more staid and always elegantly typographic.

In 1954, Monte Factor commissioned Lustig to design the logo and carton for the Diced Cream of America Company. This was a largely on-paper organization that leased franchises to manufacture Diced Cream (a low-priced ice cream with high butterfat and low air content that was never touched by human hands). Factor gave Lustig the following guidelines: "Give the product a soft, delicious look. Make the carton look as large as possible. Create gaiety, an almost sentimental use of color and design. Give a quality look that will communicate to children as well as to adults. Find the feeling of flavor freshness." And finally, "distinguish the word 'Diced' and make it slightly different than the word 'Cream.'"[54] Lustig did all those things. He combined the graphic flavors of old and new creating a "gay and quality look." He wrote to Factor "we felt that the subtle mixture of modern and old fashioned character gave the package a sense of elegance and quality that other letter forms failed to achieve."[55] Lustig also took a few liberties with the copy, including omitting the flavor from some surfaces (risky for such a product), and left out the words "flavor fresh," which he noted "are really meaningless and only clutter what is already a small surface." Despite the odd name (Diced), the packaging was compelling.

Lustig's 1947 mark for *Neurotica*, in contrast, was mind tingling, indeed somewhat menacing (see pg. 102). Edited and published by Jay Landesman between 1948 and 1951, *Neurotica* brought together some of the most original minds of the Beat generation, including Allen Ginsberg and Jack

Below left:

The Miller Company, 1950.

Two advertisements from a series.

Top right:

Gotham Carpet Company, 1952.

Advertisement.

Bottom right:

Great Ideas of Western Man, 1951.

Advertisement for The Container

Corporation of America.

Above:

Jayson, 1945.

Advertisement for a shirt company.

Opposite:

Logos by Lustig (clockwise from top):

Berzon Books, 1950.

Hokey Pokey Ice Cream, 1949.

Western Contract Manufacturers, 1940s.

Paramount Furniture, 1949.

Kerouac. The logo, also used for the premiere cover design, combined a primitive graphic line with surreal symbolism. The word *Neurotica* was ostensibly scrawled out of a black blotch, giving visual character to the psychologically disturbing title—and a perfect, cultish-looking evocation of it too.

In 1950, Lustig was commissioned by Gruen Associates, a California architectural firm headed by the Viennese architect Victor Gruen, to design the coordinated signage (main entrance and parking lot signs and water tower) for J. L. Hudson's Northland in Detroit (see pg. 172), the first American shopping mall—what *Architectural Forum* called "a new yardstick for measuring the size and quality of shopping centers."[56] It was a Modernist postwar merchandise oasis, with playful sculpture, open spaces, fountains, and gardens. Lustig had previously designed signage for other retail establishments, including Monte Factor and Sheela's women's shoe store in Beverly Hills. But Northland was incredibly complex. His logo, a Modernistic sunburst of linear rays that were emitted from a circular "N," was consistent on all the parking lot and other direction signs. It also appeared on the bulbous water tower. He used well-spaced Clarendon type to spell out Northland, rather than a more "modern" sans serif face that would have slavishly mirrored the Modernism of the buildings. He saved his sans serifs for the directional signs. Lustig continued to be interested in environmental lettering for the remainder of his life, and he provided some direction for the 1954 MoMA exhibition titled "Signs in the Street."

Opposite:
Neurotica, 1947.
Magazine cover; each issue
designed in different colors.

Right, logos from top to bottom:
Northland Shopping Center, Detroit, 1953.
Comb & Shears, 1949.
Alan Ladd (the film actor), 1949.
Monte Factor Ltd. Men's Shop, 1948.

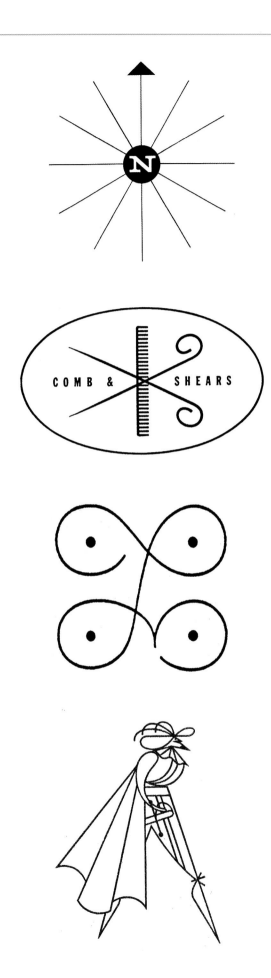

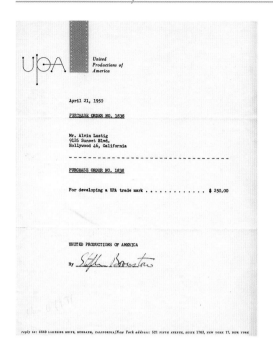

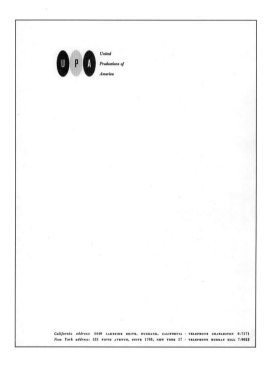

Top:

**UPA/United Productions of
America**, 1946.

Letterhead. This was a 1950 letter to
Lustig from UPA on the original 1946
design with the purchase order for
the 1950 redesign.

Bottom:

**UPA/United Productions of
America**, 1950.

Redesign of letterhead.

Despite his declining health, Lustig voraciously accepted as many commissions as possible. One demonstration of his eclecticism is that in 1953 he designed various print materials for the Girl Scouts of America and transformed aspects of their graphic identity from homespun quaintness to sophisticated modern (see pgs. 110–111). He felt that an integrated graphic design program for them would provide unified distinction. "Dynamic recognizable visual characteristic in which all the elements are related not only by certain visual features but also by a high level of formal values becomes increasing potent as a public relations device."[57]

Lustig also designed the literary journal *Perspectives* from 1952 to 1955, using nonrepresentational designs under a bold sans serif nameplate. He is further credited with the interior typographic format. By 1955, the covers were rather routine, lacking the verve of his original abstractions. In 1953, he designed startlingly symbolic covers for *Diogenes*, the journal of the Ford Foundation (see pg. 114). And that same year, he designed *Art Digest*, with a tip of the typographic hat to Jan Tschichold's signature combo of bold type. (In this case, the type consisted of a condensed slab serif *art* and a bank script *digest*. The nameplate was in a vertical white channel, while a yellow wash of color divided the image area and transparently covered a portion of the wood sculpture illustration.

ANATOMY OF A MAGAZINE COVER

A design icon doesn't come along every day. To be so considered it must not only transcend its function and stand the test of time, but also must represent the time in which it was produced. The cover of *Industrial Design*, vol. 1, no. 1, February 1954, was just such an icon. It was not just the emblem of a brand-new publishing venture and a testament to Lustig's vision, it was also, importantly, one of his last designs. Lustig was deeply involved in the design of the first two issues of the magazine and nominally with the third, as art editor, art director, and art consultant, respectively. He saw his role as the framer of ideas that were visual in nature. Although he never had the chance to develop his basic design concepts further, he left behind a modern design icon and a format that defined the magazine for years afterward.

STANLEY P. MURPHY COMPANY

DRAMATIZING PRODUCT AND SERVICE SELLING WITH MOTION PICTURES

6632 SANTA MONICA BOULEVARD, HOLLYWOOD, CALIFORNIA · HOLLYWOOD 7376

Dear Sir; This letter is typed as a suggestion
as to the best placing upon the page, in order to
enhance the design itself. As can be seen the en-
letter is organized on the line formed by the edge
of the film, making a strong left hand axis to
which all the elements conform and making it un-
necessary to try and control the right hand margin
too rigidly. The salutation is placed at the bottom in the margin.

Paragraphs are not indented, but indicated by allowing one more line space between them than is
used in the body of the letter. Double space for
a single space letter and triple for a double space
letter. The effort should be made to more or less
fill the page, using double space for short letters.
If the letter is extremely short it should be placed
high on the page rather than centered.

The closing phrase and signature should also be
placed flush with the left hand margin to keep the
entire letter balanced. The suggestions have been
made not in an effort to be merely "different" but
to produce completely designed letterhead in which
all the elements are orgnized to produce a satisfyig
combination of paper, printing and typing.

Sincerely yours

Mr. Stanley Murphy
6632 Santa Monica

COMMERCIAL FILM PRODUCTIONS · PUBLIC RELATIONS · SALES AND DEALER TRAINING · COLOR PHOTOGRAPHY · ANIMATED CARTOONS

STUDIO SET PLACEMENTS · MOTION PICTURE TIE-INS · STAR TIE-UPS · POINT-OF-PURCHASE MERCHANDISING

Above:

Stanley P. Murphy Company, 1940s.
Letterhead for film company with
typed letter to client with instructions
on placing the text on the page.

Industrial Design was the brainchild of publisher Charles Whitney, who also published the successful magazine *Interiors*. Whitney's friend George Nelson had planted the seed that the time was perfect to introduce a specialized periodical devoted to practitioners of the burgeoning field of industrial design. The year was 1953, and *Interiors* already featured an industrial design column that had evolved into a discrete section. Whitney realized that the column was a viable spinoff. *Interiors* was so smartly designed that *Industrial Design* should have similar visual panache—a coffee-table book/magazine, replete with foldouts and slip sheets, not unlike the legendary design magazine *Portfolio* (published between 1949 and 1951). And to accomplish this, an eminent art director was sought.

This was the age of great magazine art directors, including Alexey Brodovitch, Alexander Liberman, Otto Storch, Cipe Pineles, and Allen Hurlburt. Whitney believed that the magazine's design would be the deciding factor in its success. Hence Lustig, who had contributed to and was written about

in *Interiors*, was entrusted with considerable authority to design the magazine as he saw fit.

On the editorial side, however, Whitney decided to take a calculated risk by promoting two young *Interiors* associate editors to be coeditors of *Industrial Design*. Jane Fisk (later Jane Thompson of the architectural firm Thompson and Wood) and Deborah Allen may have been inexperienced in the field of industrial design, but they nevertheless had a clear plan to introduce a journalistic sensibility that emphasized criticism and analysis rather than the puff pieces common to the genre. As it turned out, this became a point of philosophical contention between the designer and editors.

If they had had a choice, the editors would have preferred an art director who, as Thompson explained, "would have been in the trenches with us," a team player with journalistic instincts rather than a distant presence with a formalist sensibility. Because Lustig designed the initial dummy and subsequent two issues in isolation in his own studio, he made certain assumptions about the presentation of content that were often inconsistent with the editors' vision. "We did not want the words to be gray space, we wanted them to have meaning," recalled Thompson about their desire for more spontaneous design responses to the material.[58] But instead of being

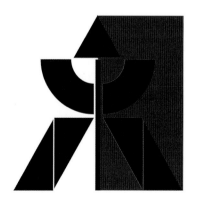

Top left:
Ralph Samuels, 1940s.
Logo for a photographer.

Bottom left:
Conference Press, 1940s.
Logo.

Clockwise from opposite top:
The Lookout, 1944.
Interoffice memo design for
Look magazine.

Abbey Bookbinders, 1940s.
Letterhead.

Mark Warnow Music, 1946.
Logo for the band leader.

The Book Stall, 1940.
Letterhead.

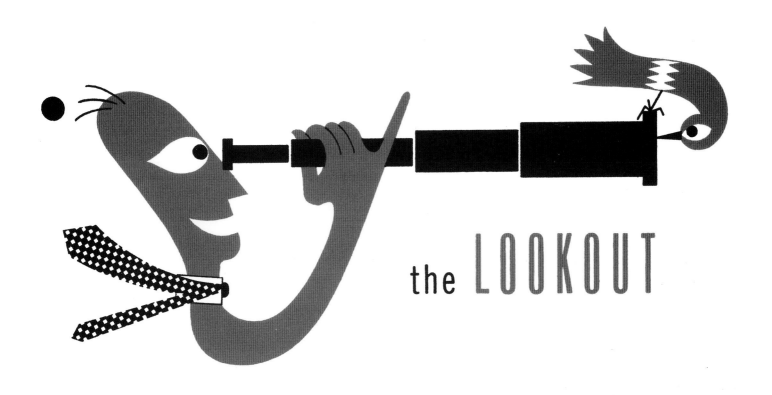

the LOOKOUT

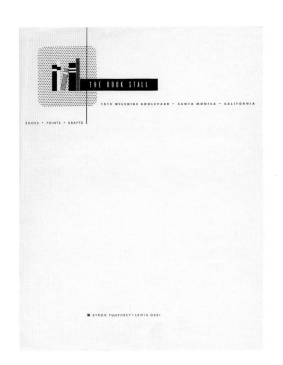

THE BOOK STALL

1515 WILSHIRE BOULEVARD · SANTA MONICA · CALIFORNIA

BOOKS · PRINTS · CRAFTS

■ BYRON PUMPHREY · LEWIS OSSI

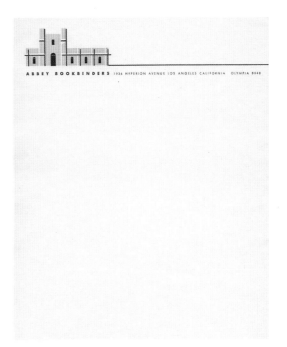

ABBEY BOOKBINDERS 1936 HYPERION AVENUE LOS ANGELES CALIFORNIA OLYMPIA 8548

Top:
***Industrial Design 3**, April 1954.
Magazine cover. Lustig also
design the interior.

Bottom:
***Industrial Design 1**, February 1954.

Opposite:
***Industrial Design 2**, March 1954.

journalistically intuitive, Lustig imposed his formal precon-
ceptions and designed the magazine as he would have a book.

Blocks of text type were indeed used as gray matter to frame
an abundance of precisely silhouetted photographs. But if it
was not as journalistically paced as, say, *Life* magazine, it was
respectfully, indeed elegantly neutral, allowing for a wide
range of material to be presented without interference. Moreover, it was what Whitney wanted; so the editors reconciled
themselves to building the magazine's editorial reputation
through informative features written by authors not previously associated with trade or professional journalism.

Thompson nevertheless disliked the first cover with its tight
grid and silhouetted photographs. Instead, she wanted to
disrupt the design purity with a few cover headlines. She
further favored a conceptual method of intersecting photography, which would convey an editorial idea, not be a pure
design. Lustig thought that cover lines would sully the design
and that intersecting photographs would be too contrived.
Years later, Thompson grudgingly admitted that Lustig's
judgment may have been wiser: "He wanted to make a
strong simple statement, which he believed [*perhaps errone-
ously since* Industrial Design *did not have to compete on the
newsstand*] had to stand up against the covers of the elegant
fashion magazines."[59] Lustig's design set the standard for
future covers, and his successor, Martin Rosenzweig, continued to produce covers for a few years afterward that more
rigidly adhered to the same formal practices. Despite these
creative tensions, the early issues of *Industrial Design* reveal
a shift in the nature of professional publishing from a trade to
cultural orientation that was underscored by Lustig's classi-
cally Modern design.

BACK TO BOOKS

During Lustig's last years, he once again reinvented book
packaging, this time with the otherwise disparaged paperback. Arthur A. Cohen, the publisher of the paperback
houses Noonday Press (founded in 1951) and Meridian
Books (founded in 1954), visited Lustig in 1952 at his studio

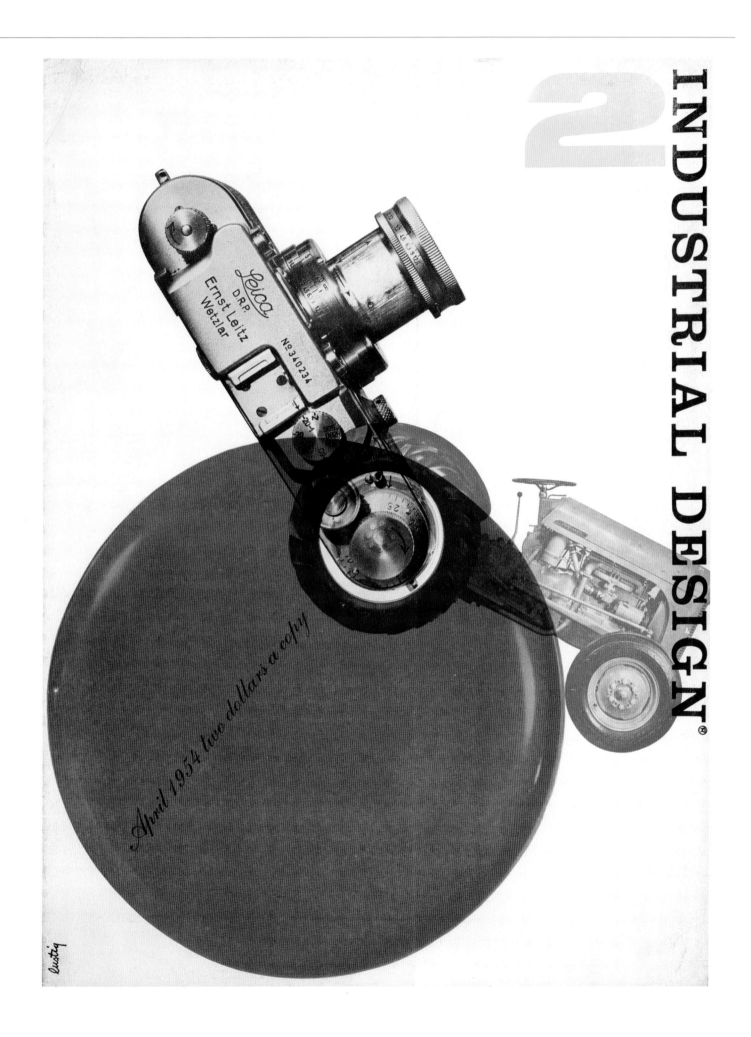

April 1954 two dollars a copy

INDUSTRIAL DESIGN

2

on Fifty-eighth Street in New York to ask him to design his line. Lustig had made a significant impression on Cohen, who wrote in *Art in America*, "It would have been quite easy for me—in deference to the conventions of the publishing industry—to have resisted the seductions of 'good design.'" Yet he learned from Lustig that design was "that most pertinent and relevant instrument of the contemporary age—a means of rediscovering old relations and refining new ones. Alvin always insisted on trying novel experiments [in his day novel]."[60] Cohen was using the paperback (and what he called the paperback revolution) as an inexpensive means of bringing literature to college students, who were plagued by high costs. Yet it wasn't until he met Lustig that he understood that his revolutionary concept needed strong packaging.

"A young publisher such as myself was characteristically prejudiced and blind," continued Cohen. "I neither felt form nor saw it. The book was simply a conventional device of communicating words in printed form. The word was all important; the book counted for little." Fortunately he was able to jettison what he called the "phony reasons" and added, "I find design neither snobbish nor pretentious, but indispensable." Like Ritchie and Laughlin, he gave considerable license to Lustig, who by 1952 was no longer interested in repeating his New Directions triumphs but rather wanted to try more simple formulations, using only typography, and much of it old Victorian, outdated faces at that. The first Noonday book covers came out in 1953, and then in 1954 the Meridian series appeared. About using the old typefaces, Cohen, who understood that being ahead of the design trends had a downside, explained, "This is not to say that Alvin's design program for Meridian Books was not a departure." Lustig's idea for Meridian books was to convince booksellers to show the paperbacks together, face out as a group, which would have the effect of lighting up the shelves. "It worked brilliantly until competition entered the paperback field and bookstores ceased to display all Meridian titles together," Cohen lamented.[61] Once Meridian's titles were separated from each other, the strength of Lustig's approach was diminished.

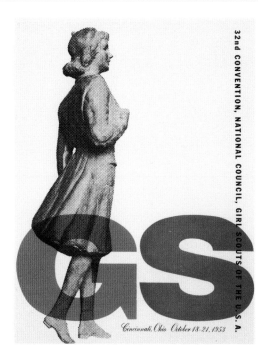

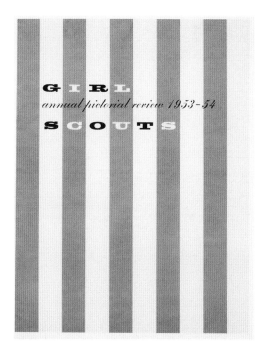

Opposite top and bottom:
I Will Try, 1954.
Brochure for Girl Scouts of America, cover and inside page.

Opposite middle:
Christmas card for Girl Scouts of America, 1954.

Top:
32nd Convention, October 18–24, 1953.
Program cover for Girl Scouts of America.

Bottom:
Annual Pictorial Review, 1954.
Cover for Girl Scouts of America.

"Since each jacket was seen in relation to each other and was envisaged by Alvin standing next to one another in the bookstore the breakup of display decreased the power and coherence of the design." Still, the covers hold up in today's market, not as unusual, but as strong, clear, and colorful.

The covers, created between 1952 and 1955, circumvented both traditional and orthodox Modern aesthetics. They served as signposts for the direction Lustig's general design had taken. At the time, American designers were obsessed with the new types being produced in Europe, not just the modern sans serifs, but re-cuts of old gothic and slab serif faces, which were difficult to obtain in the United States. Lustig had eclectic typographic tastes. He ordered specimen books from England and Germany, and he photostated and pieced together or redrew the fonts. These faces became the basis for eclectic compositions. He also became interested in, and to a certain extent adopted, the cooler (and more neutral) Swiss approach that resulted in the quieter look of the Noonday line, which did not have the same visual flair as the Meridian line.

A consideration in the design of these lines was that Lustig wanted to distinguish the books, which focused on literary and social criticism, philosophy, and history, from his New Directions fiction covers. So, he switched from pictorial imagery to pure typography set against flat color backgrounds. The typical paperback cover of that era was characterized by overly rendered illustrations or thoughtlessly composed calligraphy. Lustig's graphic economy was a counterpoint to the industry's propensity for clutter and confusion.

In 1953, Noonday Press announced that Lustig had been appointed as its design consultant. "In this capacity, he will be in charge of the complete production . . . as well as design of the catalogues and advertisements," stated a press release. "Mr. Lustig says that he will attempt to establish a distinctive style for Noonday Press books, which will try to carry out in design what Noonday has attempted to initiate in its editorial

PIANO CONCERTO IN C MAJOR, KV 467 and PIANO CONCERTO IN A MAJOR, KV 414

MOZART

The Chamber Orchestra of the Danish State Radio · FOLMER JENSEN, piano MOGENS WÖLDIKE, conductor · THE HAYDN SOCIETY/BOSTON

HSL/1054

Opposite top:
Who But You, 1947.
Cover design for Mark Warnow Sheet
Music. (Mark Warnow Band Leader)

Opposite bottom:
Joan of Arkansas, 1947.
Cover design for Mark Warnow
Sheet Music.

Clockwise from above:
Mozart,1952.

Sound Off, 1944.
Record album for Mark Warnow,
Coast Records.

Vivaldi, 1952.
Record album for Haydn Society.

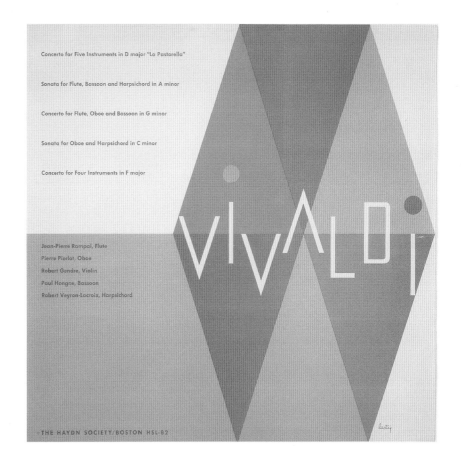

Concerto for Five Instruments in D major "La Pastorella"

Sonata for Flute, Bassoon and Harpsichord in A minor

Concerto for Flute, Oboe and Bassoon in G minor

Sonata for Oboe and Harpsichord in C minor

Concerto for Four Instruments in F major

VIVALDI

Jean-Pierre Rampal, Flute
Pierre Pierlot, Oboe
Robert Gendre, Violin
Paul Hongne, Bassoon
Robert Veyron-Lacroix, Harpsichord

THE HAYDN SOCIETY/BOSTON HSL-82

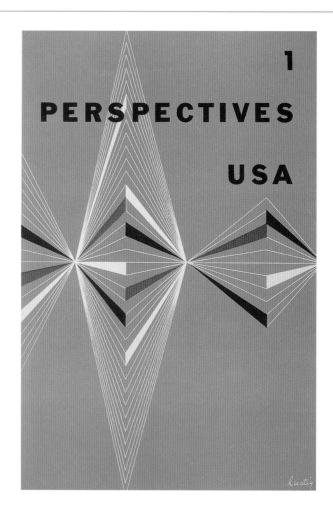

policy: 'to endeavor to publish books whose literary merit will make them a lasting possession.'" After Lustig's death, Elaine continued to design the Meridian books (Noonday had been sold to Roger Straus of Farrar, Straus and Giroux), and she ultimately married Arthur Cohen.

LIGHT AND DARKNESS

Although his vision was gradually eroding, and by 1954 he was virtually blind, Lustig continued to teach and design. After he learned that he was losing his vision, he and Elaine invited his clients to a cocktail party in order to let them know his health status and give them the opportunity to take their business to other designers. Most remained loyal. Philip Johnson even contracted with him to design the sign system for the Seagram's building after this announcement. Lustig continued to design by art-directing Elaine and his other assistants, including a young Ivan Chermayeff, in every meticulous detail to complete the work he could no longer see. He specified color by referring to the color of a chair or sofa in their house and used simple geometries to express his mental pictures.

Lustig refused to resign himself to his fate. During the very last year of his life (1954–55), an enormous amount of print work flowed successfully through the studio. In addition to Meridian covers, Lustig produced three art catalogs for MoMA, a catalog for Consolidated Vacuum Corporation, a brochure for Squibb, invitations for Jacques Seligmann Gallery, jackets for *Industrial Design in America 1954* and *The Growth of the Book Jacket* by Charles Rosner, and, with Elaine, the Lightolier Christmas card and a rental brochure for Cushman & Wakefield.

As an oeuvre, Lustig's print work reveals an evolution from an experimental to mature practice, from total abstraction to symbolic imagery to expressive typography. One cannot help but wonder about how he would have continued had he lived past his fortieth year.

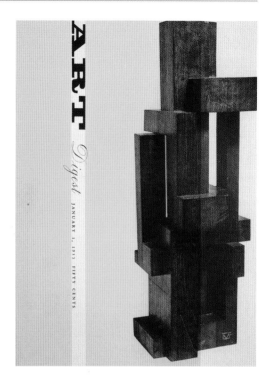

Clockwise from opposite top left:
Diogenes, 1953.
Magazine cover (Lustig also designed interior typography).

Perspectives USA, No 1, 1952.
Magazine cover (Lustig also designed interior typography).

Gentry, 1952.
Magazine cover.

Fortune, September 1952.
Magazine cover.

Above:
Art Digest, January 1, 1953.
Magazine cover.

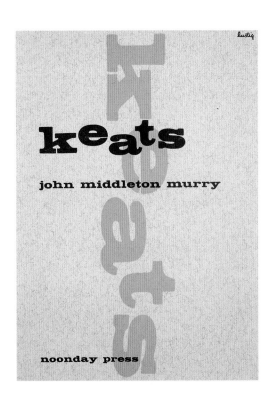

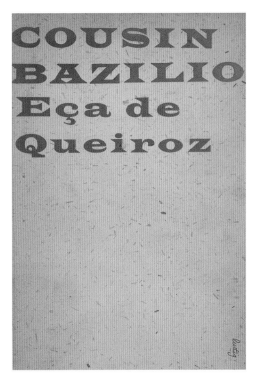

Clockwise from top left:
Keats, 1953.
Book cover, Noonday Press.

Imperialism & Social Classes, 1954.
Paperback book cover, Meridian Books.

Cousin Bazilio, 1953.
Book cover, Noonday Press.

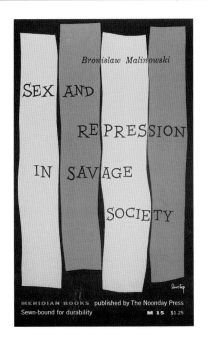

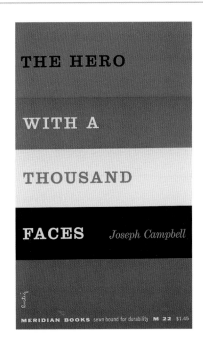

Meridian Books paperback
covers 1954–55.

Clockwise from top left:
Sex and Repression in Savage Society

The Hero with a Thousand Faces

Pragmatism

Shakespearean Tragedy

The Man of Letters in the Modern World

Byzantine Civilization

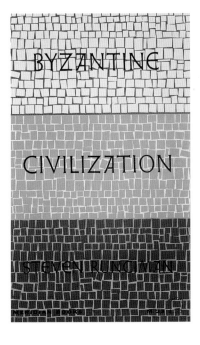

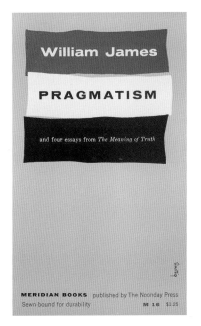

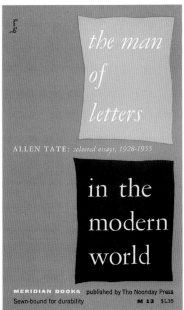

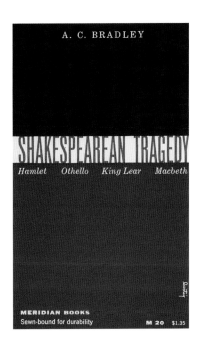

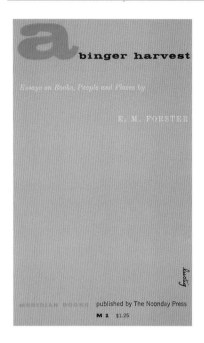

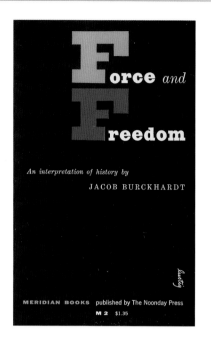

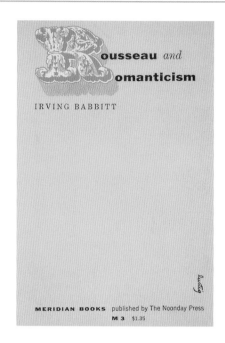

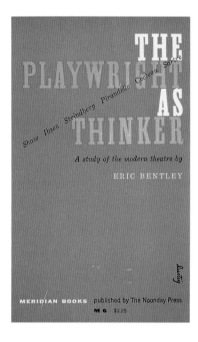

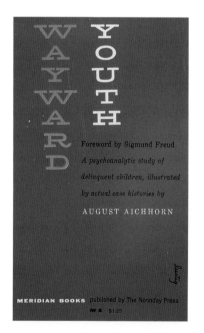

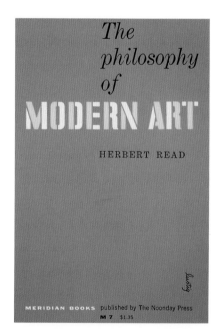

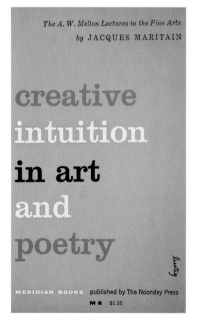

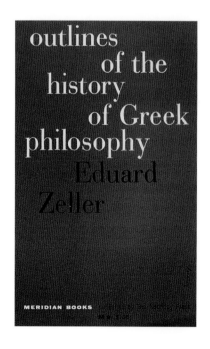

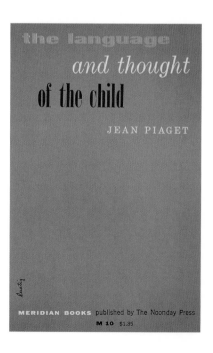

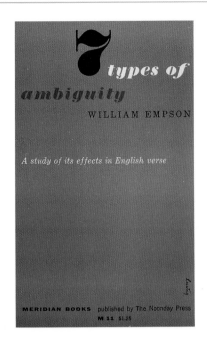

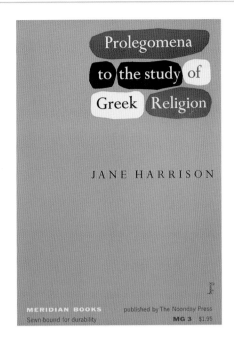

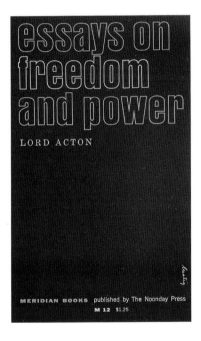

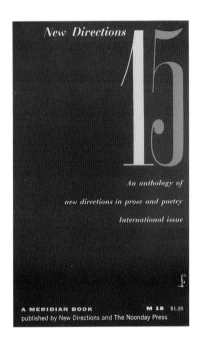

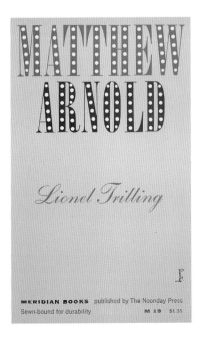

Meridian Books in which Lustig used old wood and metal types to establish an identity.

Opposite top from left:
Abinger Harvest

Force and Freedom

Rousseau and Romanticism

Opposite middle from left:
The Playwright as Thinker

Wayward Youth

The Philosophy of Modern Art

Opposite bottom from left:
Creative Intuition in Art and Poetry

Outlines of the History of Greek Philosophy

The Languge and Thought of the Child

This page clockwise from top left:
7 Types of Ambiguity

Prolegomena to the Study of Greek Religion

New Directions 15

Medieval Panorama

Matthew Arnold

Essays on Freedom and Power

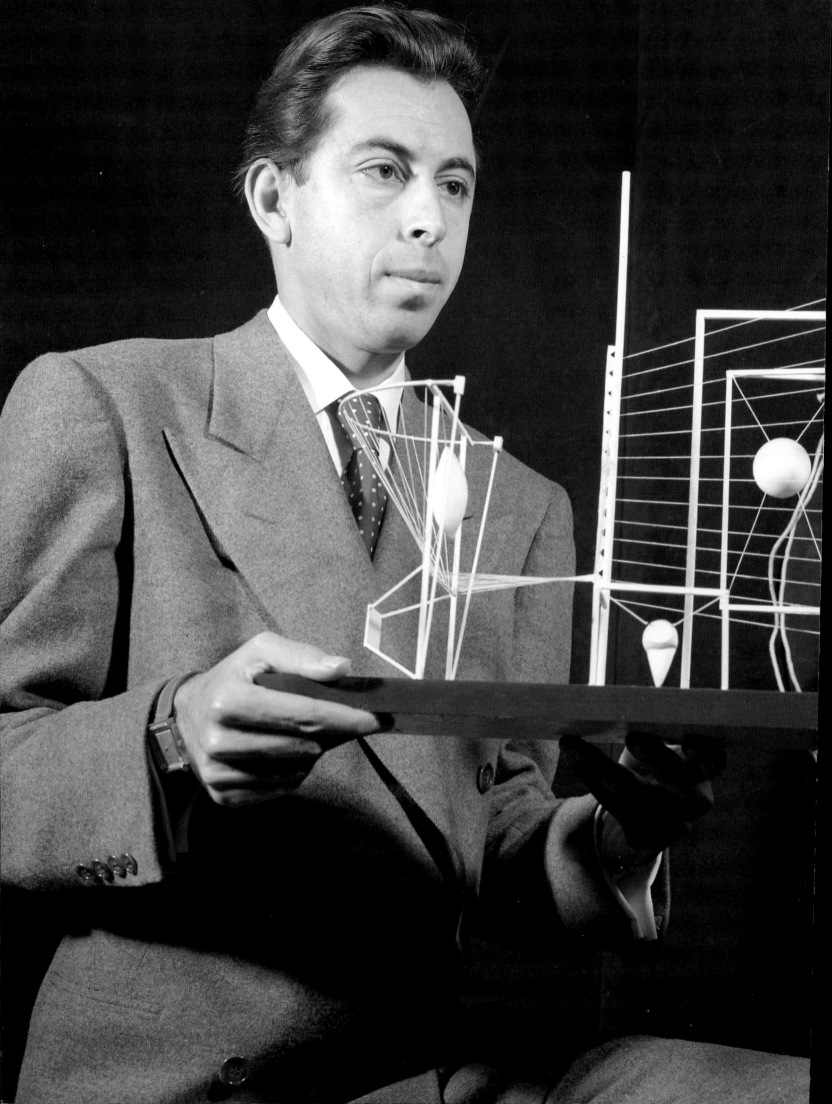

BUILDING MODERN
A Three-Dimensional World

ARCHITECTURE, INTERIORS, AND FURNITURE

Alvin Lustig was exceptionally photogenic. Poised and handsome, like a Hollywood movie star, he projected a confident aura, the quintessence of the well-designed designer. One of the most alluring of his many photographs (right) shows the dapper thirty-two-year-old leaning against the narrow doorway to his 9126 Sunset Boulevard, Los Angeles, studio under a sign with "Alvin Lustig" painted in neatly letter-spaced Bodoni. Behind him is the fabric "Incantation," a field of linear glyphs. Casual in posture but formal in demeanor, Lustig was the youthful impresario, his studio a stage on which Modernism was performed. "Incantation" was a curtain pulled back on the California Modern movement.

This photographic glimpse into Lustig's work space reveals a vibrant alternative to the piece-goods look of the typical "art service" studio. Yet an even closer reading of the image suggests that Lustig was primed to radically alter the way design impacted the public; his office was the nerve center of a newly integrated discipline. Lustig was committed to integration in the broadest sense. "In our fragmented times we must seek for wholeness," he wrote in an undated draft of a speech.[62] "For the artist the primary problem is to find some balance between his own personal creative integrity and the still undefined wants of society." Lustig was ardently rejecting design specialization "as deadening to the field as to the designer."

He tried his hand at furniture, industrial design, and what was then being called "sculpture for architecture," environmental signage for the Northland Shopping Center in Detroit. (He also designed a ten-foot-high steel garden sculpture for a doctor that prompted further inquiries from other potential private clients.) *Interiors* magazine noted in 1953, "the scope and scale of his California output would be impressive even if he had never designed a fabric or helicopter or interior; several shops, a hotel and an apartment house were the major, but by no means only, monuments of the period."[63] The work he did in New York, while not as monumental in scale, was nonetheless significant. The publisher William Segal was described in *Interiors* with various superlatives: "A brilliant harlequinade, red and black diamonds on a panel, focuses attention from a long foyer to the living room. Behind it, the vanishing point of the hallway perspective, is a Gothic Madonna enshrined on a panel of gold leaf [the façade of an elevated cupboard]. Lustig was very fond of his skewed perspective technique. The path of the entry is continued by a mock partition of beaded strings. Like a shower of colored raindrops, it makes a foreground through which to size up the room beyond. An elegant lighting strategy, U-tubes cradling fluorescent lights, defines the upper plane of the room by penning a giant T overhead."[64] The whole composition is extremely impressive for someone who has been viewed primarily as a graphic designer and typographer.

Interiors reported that during his years in New York (1951–1955), Lustig continued to work "with equal facility in two and three dimensions," and dealt "in a single day with such diverse clients as Miller Lighting Company [advertising], Noonday Press [complete design of a series of books], American Crayon Company [exhibition design], and the Girl Scouts [all publications]." Add to this various interior design projects that "often have a delicate painterly quality, which is part of his style; yet the furniture or ornament he designs linearly never fails to become part of a sculptural whole."[65]

Lustig was ambivalent about decoration. Four walls were not just bare canvases to be swathed with ornament. He saw three-dimensional space as a container for "graphic divertissements," for objects in a room that had meaning and resonance. "His ornament," wrote *Interiors*, "has the honest artificiality of man-made art, and never pretends to be anything else. It is a visual focus, or series of foci, introduced into a room for diversion and excitement." This impulse to control his total environment began when, as a teenager, he designed his own bedroom. As has been described earlier, he developed a mastery of space by designing each and every one of his studios as testament to his Modernist ardor.

The commercial and residential interiors Lustig designed for himself and others reflect the postwar design epoch in most celebrated of the late Modern architects. His design for the interior and exterior of the chic Sheela's shoe store (see pgs. 140–141) in Los Angeles was imbued with postwar optimism. For the guest rooms at the Beverly Carlton Hotel in Beverly Hills, he created an air of cheerful luxury. In addition, the offices and apartments he designed were never ad hoc or predigested schemes. He had his preferences, but for many spaces he devised custom tables, chairs, drapes, lighting fixtures, and wall coverings that emphasized functionally appropriate simplicity. And while these rooms were routinely photographed without any people in them as a way to highlight Lustig's formalism, it is clear that they were designed entirely with human beings in mind. Comfort, he proved, was attainable through modern means.

•

Page 120:
Art Center College advertising design instructor Alvin Lustig holding a 3D model, circa 1947. Photo © Art Center College of Design.

•

Page 123:
Lustig's first work space, Los Angeles, 1942–1943.

•

Opposite and above:
Lustig's first work space in the early '40s. This single room was used as his living and working space. The Precolumbian figure (this page) appears in all his offices.

Opposite and top:
Lustig's office while visual research
director at *Look* magazine, New York,
1944.

Bottom:
The office entryway with photogram
by Herbert Matter.

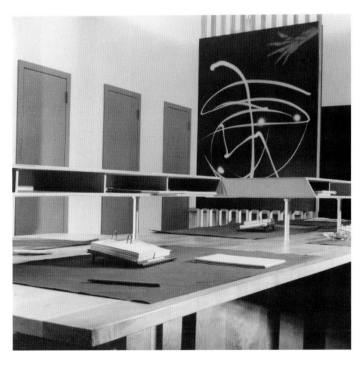

●

Opposite top and bottom:
More views of Lustig's office at *Look*
magazine, New York, 1944.

●

Top:
Lustig's office in Beverly Hills, 1946.

Bottom:
Elevation drawing of the office, 1946.

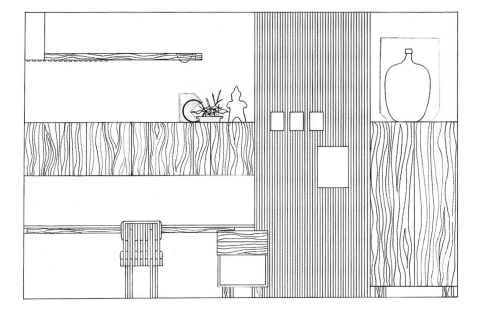

Lustig believed that a work space was a showroom that should express a designer's uniqueness. His own 1947 Los Angeles office revealed a total immersion in Modern art. His private workroom was an array of harmonious Modern forms. The desk, with its economical linearity and cantilevered drawers, was inspired by contemporary architecture. The chairs were derived from a Modern template. Even the floors were grid paintings reminiscent of Piet Mondrian, with alternately colored intersecting lines that echoed the linear quality of the back wall, which was itself composed of parallel lines interrupted by a dark panel lightheartedly marked with numerical measurements. On the opposite white wall, an enlargement of one of Lustig's "Incantation" glyphs contrasted with small African and pre-Columbian figures. Mexican straw baskets were used to punctuate the otherwise pure geometric quality of the room. (These accessories were found in all his dwellings.) Incidentally, but not inconsequentially, Lustig's desk was characteristically free from any messy artist's materials,

save for pen, pencil, and pad of paper. This was not affectation for the photographer; Lustig was as fastidious about his environment as he was about his attire.

Lustig was uncanny when it came to fitting more into less space. This was the principle tenet of his 1945 Beverly Hills office design. The lack of space was his main problem, but he mediated it through the airy quality of the furniture he selected and designed. Rich-grained Central American mahogany of honey hue by the cabinetmaker Manuel Sandoval, a Frank Lloyd Wright protégé, provided the studio with its necessary focal points. Lustig's lamps provided indirect lighting for the desks, with black enameled reflectors set into a frame eighteen inches below the ceiling. A wall cabinet not only provided storage off the floor but held the desk lights. A salt and pepper rug and brown-gray, yellow, and white walls gave the space an earthy look. For this office, Lustig devised an innovative display system; he attached a standard steel tool that supported

mounted displays that snapped between decorative wood strips. On these he hung book jackets and advertisements, which seemed to float on the wall.

Although he rejected nonessentials in the Bauhaus tradition, Lustig should not be confused with dogmatic minimalists. His 1943 Los Angeles office, an apartment that included a kitchen and two small rooms, was replete with the objects that signaled his proclivity for visual play, including a terra-cotta pre-Columbian figurine and a reproduction of a Rousseau painting. Nothing was without purpose. The floor-to-ceiling drapes opposite a brick fireplace gave the illusion of more livable area than there really was. A dark floor with lighter throw rugs gave the impression of higher ceilings. The overall effect was of a comfortable "living" room, rather than solely a working room.

Opposite:
Reporter Publications, New York, 1945.
William Segal's desk.

Above:
Reporter Publications office, with work-station partitions.

●
Above:
Another view of Reporter
Publications office.

●
Opposite top and bottom:
Lustig's office, Los Angeles, 1947.

In 1944, Lustig was hired as the visual research director of *Look* magazine, in New York, where he developed the design and produced the content for *Staff*, the in-house publication. It was agreed before he took the job that he would also design his own office suite. At the time, he was experimenting with the spatial concept he called a fluid environment. Traditional offices in the same streamlined, set-back Madison Avenue building were usually characterized by blocky wood desks, high-back leather-upholstered chairs, and imposing hardwood bookcases. Lustig designed one-off furniture that gave the impression that it floated on air (by virtue of standing on thin legs). The photographs taken by Lustig's friend, the surrealist filmmaker Maya Deren, reveal an environment framed by linear masses; it was free of conventional sedentary dividers and other such encumbrances. Lustig enjoyed toying with contrasts. Glass tables and vases were placed on light and dark wood surfaces; open shelves alternated with closed cabinets; dark wood panels on which lights were hung from the ceiling contrasted with the light-colored painted walls, which varied in hue from wall to wall. Even a Herbert Matter photomural that hung in the main work area was a blend of contrasting representational and abstract forms. Everything about the office encouraged, if not symbolized, the fluidity of the creative process.

Lustig understood that an office could not be a pristine or unfettered environment. As the designer, he could never have the last word on how the space would ultimately function in the real world. Nor could he control the degree of wear and tear that would take its toll on his design. He could only hope that the quality of the design contributed to a vital (and comfortable) workplace. In 1945, Lustig fine-tuned his "open plan" when he designed the offices for Reporter Publications in New York. He believed the open setting, so popular today with architects like Renzo Piano, encouraged creative interaction. Reporter Publications had a decidedly cramped space in the Empire State Building. The problem for Lustig, noted an article in *Architectural Forum*, was "fitting an oversized staff into undersized work space"—only forty by forty feet for twenty-two employees.[66] Lustig had to use every inch

Top:
Lustig's 58th St. office entrance,
New York, 1952.

Bottom:
Drawing of the light fixture above
Lustig's desk.
It was inexpensive to have a metal craftsman create the shape on which you could
clip common flood lamps with their cords,
eliminating the need for elaborate wiring.

Opposite:
Lustig's personal office, with light fixture,
New York, 1952.

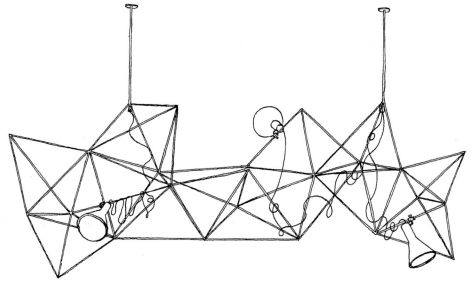

Top, left and right:
Views of Lustig's 58th St. office,
New York, 1952.

Bottom:
Lustig's 58th St. office separation
between entryway and assistants' work
space. The slats were white with a few
random colors. When a visitor walked
in, Lustig was on the right; he wanted to
separate the tiny work space from the
public. There was a receptionist, and
the hanging screen separated the studio
working space. Lustig's office was down
the hall in a separate room.

of available space, and do this without making the sedentary staff members too claustrophobic. He "dissolved solidity wherever possible while still retaining some sense of privacy." Doors were completely omitted; work areas were defined only by intersecting and curling screen walls. Lustig's most novel idea involved a system of direct and indirect lighting, coming from sconces with mushroomlike lamps that bounced light off reflecting disks to the desks below. He designed these himself. Glass walls and glass-topped desks provided a further sense of transparency and fluidity. Throughout the space, small personal touches, such as area rugs and straw waste baskets, afforded more nuanced intimacy.

There was no better example of Lustig's facility to maximize the limitations of space than the office that he designed for himself in 1952 in an otherwise grungy walk-up building on Manhattan's East Fifty-eighth Street. Elaine Lustig Cohen recalled: "It was absolutely hideous. In the first hour we ripped it apart and cleaned it up." As was the case in his other spaces, none of the furniture, not even the flat files, sat boulderlike on the floor. All the furnishings were elevated by small legs or open shelves, and in addition to the structural walls, Lustig devised a wooden blind (actually more like a slatted fence), that hung from the ceiling. It both separated the reception from the work areas and allowed for transparency. A beaded curtain, one of his favorite quirky conceits, replaced the door on the storeroom. While he used certain existing seating (he particularly favored Eames chairs) and lamps, he designed custom, sculptural lighting fixtures that looked very similar to a few of the abstract linear designs on his book jackets. The main feature, however, was his own office, which included floor-to-ceiling drapes (to help smooth out the edges of the room) and his legendary marble desk.

For his home, Lustig used similarly startling yet playful devices. London's *Architectural Design* magazine reported that his apartment revealed "clarity and simplicity of form strongly allied to the great representation effect achieved in his graphic art by the simplest of means."[67] The magazine was referring to a door grill through which the interior of the apartment appears as though in a halftone photograph. Lustig's design for an upholstered winged chair, originally created for the Paramount Furniture Co., is noteworthy in the contrast between the softly molded seat and back and the severe, decisive lines of the metal carriage. These linear motifs are also akin to the abstract forms he used in certain printed work.

Predictably, all his work had a graphic underpinning either in the shape of line or pattern of the fabric. In fact, Lustig did not consider himself an interior designer at all. "If you asked him what lamps to buy for your living room," explained Elaine Lustig Cohen, "he would say, 'I can't tell you what lamp to buy, but I'll redo the living room for you.' That was the way he handled all his commissions. Clients let him do what he wanted."[68] Whether he designed three-dimensional spaces in the same way that he designed two-dimensional book covers, magazines, and catalogs is ultimately irrelevant. Everything he designed had the same relevance and aim for permanence. Yet if there was a professional hierarchy, it was that the workplace was primary, and the art and design grew out of the aesthetically inspiring environment.

Although he is not thought of today as an industrial designer, Lustig's work was respected in that field. Walter Landor, the San Francisco brand and industrial designer, urged Lustig in a 1948 letter "to go through your file of photographs of Lustig-designed architecture, furniture, interiors, etc. even possibly fabrics and graphic stuff and send me a selection that I might use in *Architects' Yearbook*."[69] Landor was preparing a review of West Coast architecture since the war. "Being you are one of the few who can express themselves, it might be good to have your ideas on where you stand in relation to other practitioners, and have your views on good and bad trends inherent in the work currently being done here on the Coast."

Ben Charles interior, Los Angeles,
1946.

Above:
Wood sculpture over the fireplace.

Opposite:
Two views of the Ben Charles
living room.

CALIFORNIA DREAMING

Lustig's architectural sensibility was synonymous with the
Southern California zeitgeist. California's motion picture
and oil industries were on the upswing, and architects like
Rudolph Schindler, Richard Neutra, Julius Ralph Davidson,
and Frank Lloyd Wright's son, Lloyd Wright, were building
emblematic structures. Lustig's friendships with architects, most notably Richard Neutra, and patrons of arts and
culture, like Galka Scheyer, Walter and Louise Arensberg,
and Billy Wilder, influenced his views and inspired his practice. His work for John Entenza's *Arts & Architecture*, even
though it ended on a sour note, was still an important connection for him. Although he lived his final years in New York,
his heart belonged to California. He extolled it for its "sense
of exhilaration and growth that charges the very air."[70] The
region was particularly well suited for the development of
modern architecture: "The climate, the freedom from tradition, the heightened sense of life—all these factors contribute
to make a unique architectural opportunity," he continued.
Unfortunately, while he saw California as fertile ground, he
admitted that it was a hectic "scrambling of clichés and ill-
digested forms. The quality in our environment which gives
us freedom also limits us by failing to impose discipline."

In addition to store and residence designs in Beverly Hills,
including Sheela's, Monte Factor, Henry Weiss Studio, and
Frank Perls Gallery, Lustig worked on complete buildings.
Although he did not have a formal architectural education
or license, his instincts were keen. "Lustig strives for vital
compression of line and form," waxed *Los Angeles Times* art
critic and close friend, Jules Langsner, in an undated draft for
an article, "compression that balances a maximum of weight
with effortless poise. By the use of subtle color relationships
and linear inventiveness, Lustig's compression provokes
our interest in addition to satisfying our functional needs . . .
Thus in his architecture Lustig is not content to functionally enclose a volume but seeks to give that enclosure a linear
configuration."[71]

Opposite:

Sheela's, Beverly Hills, 1947.
Storefront for women's accessory shop.

Top:

Sheela's, Beverly Hills, 1947.
Interior design.

Bottom:

Sheela's, Beverly Hills, 1947.
Letterhead.

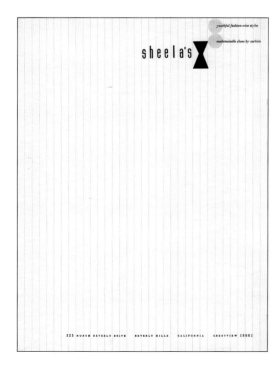

●

Top:

Monte Factor, Ltd. Beverly Hills, 1947.
Store design for men's clothing shop.

Middle and bottom:

Monte Factor, Ltd. Beverly Hills, 1947.
Announcement card and gift boxes.

●

Opposite:

Monte Factor, Ltd. Beverly Hills, 1947.
Interior design with division panel
and logo.

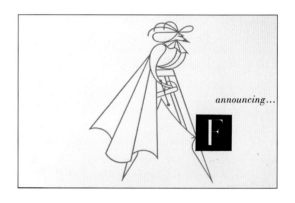

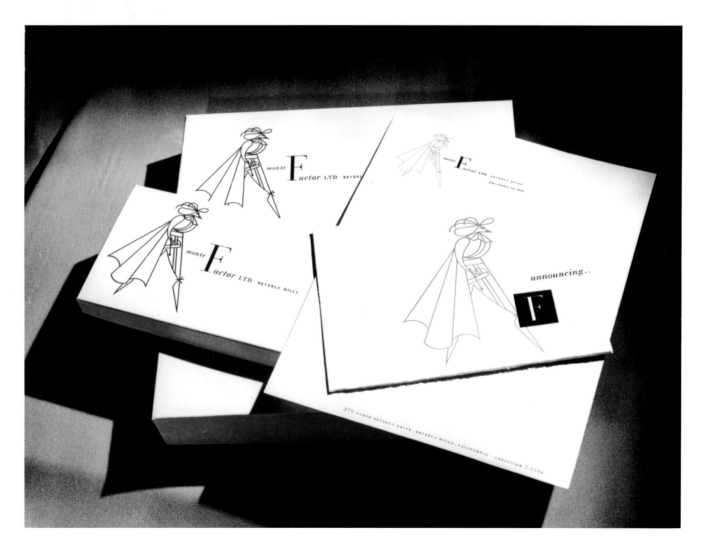

With Sam Reisbord (1904–1985), known for designing his
share of late-Modern hotels, Lustig designed the Beverly
Carlton Hotel (1947–1948), a luxury apartment house, the
Beverly Landau (1947–1948), and the Institute of Jewish Education for the Zionist labor movement. He designed a house
for the artist June Wayne (1949), and with Edgardo Contini,
an engineer and founding partner of Gruen Associates, he
created the Concrete Pavilion project in Los Angeles. The
pavilion was an experiment in the use of reinforced concrete
as a surface tension material, for which Lustig designed the
structure and a mural affixed to it.

Although it was never completed, Lustig was commissioned
in the early '40s to design a new home for film director Billy
Wilder, from whom he received a rent-free studio in the
garage of his home on North Beverly Drive. His relationship
with Wilder was of the true patron to willing artist. "Just to
show you what kind of guy he is," Lustig wrote in an undated
letter to James Laughlin, "I am to spend up to $200 for any
architectural books that I think might interest him. . . ." At
the outset, the project was on a good trajectory, but Lustig
wrote, "I think I frighten him just a bit. He is not sure if I
am a genius or a screwball. He thinks he wants what I want
but he gulps and swallows sometimes. He is a wonderful
guy. . . ."[72] Lustig's plans nonetheless stalled, and Charles
and Ray Eames (whom Lustig introduced to Wilder) were
commissioned to design a 4,600-square-foot house for a
hilltop locale above Sunset Boulevard. The house was to be the
epitome of Modernism, sleek and airy, almost totally glass.
But Wilder's wife, Audrey, decided she couldn't be bothered
with the upkeep and put an end to the folly.

Southern California was an oasis where sun, light, air, vista,
and natural growth were abundant; this underpinned Lustig's
distinct California aesthetic. His favorite color, terra-cotta,
was employed often. Yet as he argued in the *Design* article,
"no matter how wondrous the physical opportunities are,
without a clear understanding of the basic principles and even
conflicts inherent in the movement, nothing but architectural
hash will be produced." He added that the prevalent willingness to "try anything," instead of becoming a liberating force,
often produces only a form of architectural sensationalism.

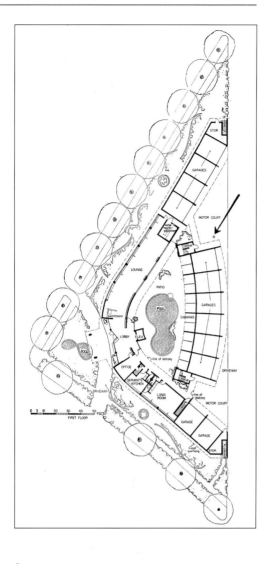

Opposite:
Weiss Jewery Shop,
Beverly Hills, 1947.

Above:
Beverly Carlton Hotel,
Los Angeles, 1948.
Architectural ground plan.

145

Top and opposite:
Beverly Carlton Hotel,
Los Angeles, 1948.
Front entrance of the building
and interior courtyard.

Beverly Carlton Hotel,
Los Angeles, 1948.
Interior courtyard.

"We are in danger of producing a sterile and barren architecture . . . In our anxiety to appear sufficiently 'rich' we camouflage our bad skeletons with endless textures and materials. Poor craftsmanship, paucity of imagination and an inability to think simply and structurally are covered with a heavy gravy of surface effects." Lustig warned against the novelty and faux historical architecture that emerged throughout Los Angeles and the environs. Carrying the design cudgel, he sought to mobilize young designers like himself who had "the great opportunity to inherit" modern beliefs, ideas, and discoveries. "If we are going to develop an architecture worthy of the terrain and the potential living pattern, we must be stern in our self-criticism. . . ."[73]

Lustig's self-education about architecture, and by extension city planning, was stimulated by some of the books he designed.

In 1942, planner Mel Scott wrote *Cities Are for People: The Los Angeles Region Plans for Living*, which Lustig designed. It was an analysis of proposals for Los Angeles that exuded a sense of optimism based on single-family homes, spacious boulevards, and broad freeways. Lustig also designed the very sprightly *A Guide to Contemporary Architecture in Southern California* (1951), which was intended to make the state appear futuristic, and *American Woods* (1951), which focused on wood as a resilient building material. His interest in structures and materials would continue through his career.

Lustig was highly critical of sensationalist California architecture, yet nonetheless cheerful when discussing how ripe California was for industrial design and the new industrial designer. "Before the war the logical field for the industrial designer was largely the East," he wrote in *Western Advertising*.

"Now he can find in the West, perhaps not the great concentrations of industrial power, but more stimulating opportunities. There is a freshness and experimental attitude that cannot be found in the more tradition shackled East."[74] He wrote about how he saw his own role in industrial design. Rather than restyling existing products, his task and that of others in California was more frequently to create new ones. Western industry, and by extension, Lustig's industriousness, was "free to lead the way in visual appeal and consumer convenience."

From 1946 to 1948, Lustig ("brilliant stylist of modern stores, shops and specialized structures" stated an ad for the program in *Arts & Architecture*) brought industrial design to Art Center with a special program. He exerted great influence on his students, who were attending Art Center and the California School of Art on the GI Bill, including John Follis, Rex Goode,

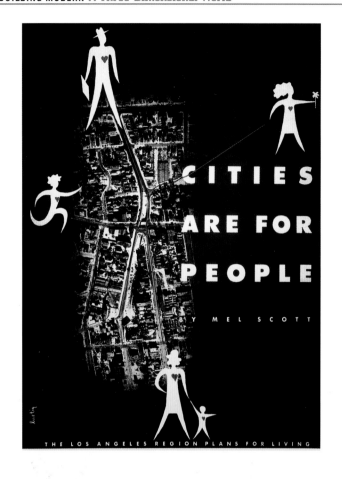

Clockwise from opposite top left:
Cities Are for People, 1942.
Paperback cover and inside
spread designed for L.A. City
Planning Commission.

**A Guide to Contemporary Architecture
In Southern California**, 1949.
Book cover and the entire
spiral-bound book.

**Metropolitan Los Angeles,
One Community**, 1949.
Book cover and the entire
book design.

Above:
Beverly Landau Apartments,
Los Angeles, 1948.
Entrance.

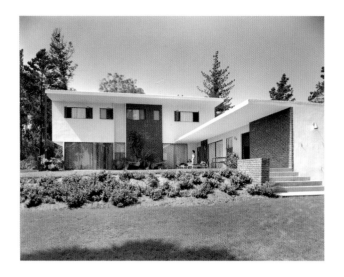

Above:

June Wayne house, 1949.
Lustig designed the interior and exterior.

Opposite top:

Roteron Helicopter, 1945.
Designed for the Roteron Instrument
Company owned by Lustig's friend
William Thomas, who also owned
Lansing Speakers.

Opposite bottom:

Preliminary drawing for the Roteron
helicopter.

Frederick Usher, and Louis Danziger, several of whom became significant graphic designers. Lustig's overarching belief in the complete work of art was impressed upon them.

By then, industrial design was fixed in Lustig's repertoire. In 1944, Lustig designed a single-seat, midget helicopter for the Roteron Company. The commission came from William H. Thomas, a close friend (they met at Los Angeles City College) and brilliant engineer who had hired Lustig to design a brochure for Kittell-Muffler in 1939. The key to the Roteron helicopter's engineering efficiency was the placement of the engine between two coaxial rotors, allowing more space in the fuselage and a savings in construction costs. It sold retail for $2,800. Lustig designed the shell to have the air of lightness, grace, and economy. The cab was made of two pieces of molded plywood, scarf-joined down the center. Plastic windows were hinged to the continuous steel tubing. Ultimately, aluminum was used for the skin. The futuristic design was reminiscent of Lustig's graphic abstractions but totally functional. That he had the temerity to design something so alien to his practice was evidence of his self-confidence and understanding of total design.

Thomas later went on to build upon the work of James B. Lansing, founder of Lansing Sound company (also famously known as JBL). He refined the transducer product line and produced speaker systems for which Lustig also designed graphics. Thomas admired Lustig's ability to focus on the core of a problem. "He would not waste any words on you if he felt you weren't interested," Thomas is quoted as saying in a remembrance. "But if you demonstrated genuine interest in design, he would spend all the time in the world to explain the aesthetics and subjective significance of what he was trying to do."[75] Lustig designed many of the early graphic pieces that explained JBL's products. Arguably, the Thomas-Lustig collaboration was key to the early success of the company. Lustig was also quite a booster for progressive furniture and fabric design. In 1945, he made his first sketch for Cohama, a textile that was never produced. In 1947, Lustig's emblematic "Incantation" was released by Laverne Originals. Two

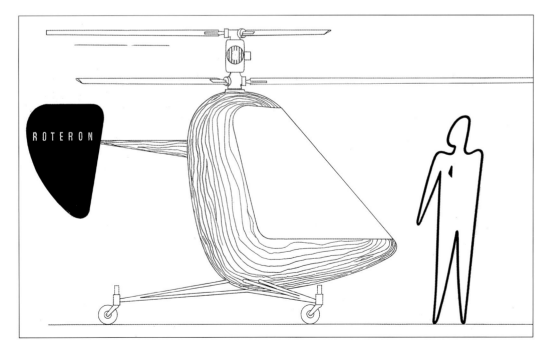

Top:

Lustig chair designed for Paramount
Furniture, 1949.
Custom upholstered chair produced
on order.

Bottom:
Sketches for hanging light fixtures,
1953. (Never produced.)

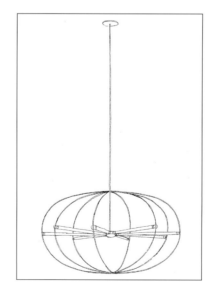

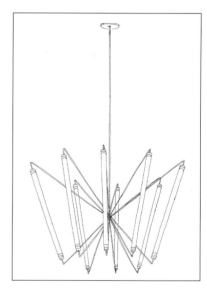

Left:

Lamp, 1949.
Custom standing lamp design
for Edgardo Contini.

Right top and bottom:
Sketches for hanging light
fixtures, 1953.
(Never produced.)

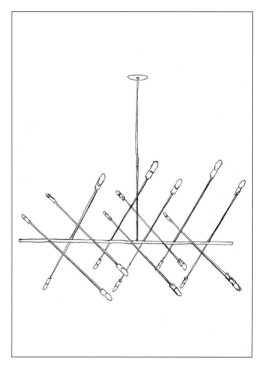

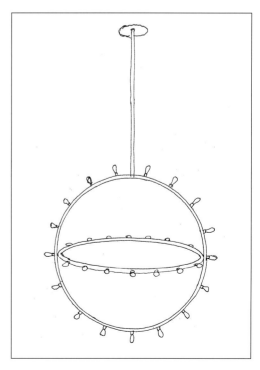

Opposite:
Lustig in his Los Angeles office, 1947.

Top:
Garden sculpture, Beverly Hills, 1950.
Designed for a doctor.

Bottom:
Architectural project, 1949.
Concrete shelter designed with
Edgardo Contini.

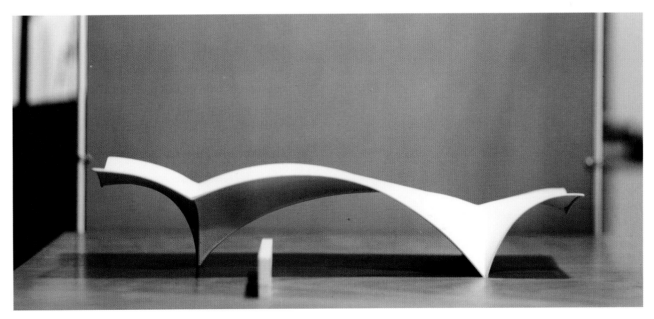

●

Above:

Incantation Fabric, 1947.

Lustig's office entrance, Los Angeles.

●

Opposite left:

Counterchange, 1949.

Fabric design for L. Anton Maix Fabrics.

Opposite right:

Incantation, 1947.

Fabric design for Laverne Originals.

years later, he created two additional fabric patterns for L. Anton Maix. That same year, his upholstered chair (also called "The Lustig Chair") for Paramount (see pg. 152) went on sale (about fifty of them were made), and he designed a standing light for Edgardo Contini (see pg. 153). Lustig viewed modern furniture and fabric design as a significant benefit for people. It was good to live with good design. Yet he railed in notes for a 1953 speech that prior to the Modern movement, furniture design was generally in the hands of "company designers" employed by large industrialized manufacturers who were "rarely more than skilled combiners of tradition and fashion and almost never possessed any genuine understanding of the principles of creative design."[76] At the time, "furniture design of any merit" was designed by contemporary architects for their own use "after failing to find anything acceptable in the regular market." But by the early '50s, large mass-production furniture companies were luring the "name" designer, whereas they would have "ignored him only a few years ago." Lustig attributed this upsurge in design consciousness to be the result of a younger generation seeking "symbols of vitality that could not be found in the old traditional forms of their parents." He also noted that a vast army of publicists, merchandisers, and tastemakers sensed the "vitality and potential growth of 'modern' and have thrown the full weight of their machinery in its favor." Nonetheless, Lustig was always wary of the "superficial devotee either as a designer, producer or consumer" who makes possible a "great wave of mediocrity in the name of design."

In *American Fabrics*, Lustig wrote about a new wave "initiated by people outside of the fabric industry, such as architects or their wives, furniture designers, interior designers, graphic designers, and sometimes painters or sculptors. They all understood the principles of modern design in one or more fields and sought to achieve the same result in fabrics."[77] This was a field in which Lustig, had he lived, would have pushed the conventions.

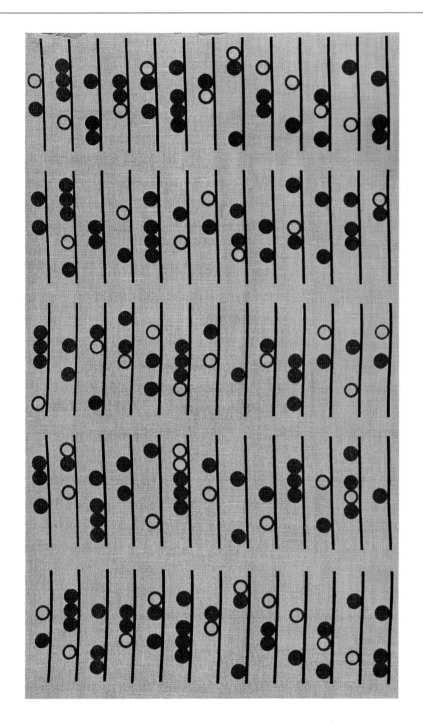

Opposite:

Intaglio, 1949.

Fabric design for L. Anton Maix Fabrics.

Above:

Lustig interior, 1951–1952.

Living room in Lustron house rental,

Croton-on-the Hudson.

Yet how his innovation would have fared can only be guessed at. Incantation, which was made as a textile and as wallpaper, actually sold very poorly. "I am unhappy that we have not done well with the design in view of all our promotion and advertising," wrote Erwin Laverne, owner of Laverne Originals. "Personally, I think that Incantation is one of the most beautiful modern prints being made today, and I say that, not because you designed it and we are printing it, but because I really believe it. I think it's going to take a little more time, but so far it has been disappointing and surprising that with all our effort it has not gone over."[78]

Lustig's forays into furniture were not always satisfying either. Nor did he design as much furniture as he would have wanted. Nonetheless, he was looking forward to greater opportunities in the future. "There is a feeling among the

more mature and creative of the furniture designers that we are in a period of consolidation and a phrase that was often used at the recent International Design Conference in Aspen, Colorado was 'a moratorium of invention,'" he wrote.[79] Yet he also stated that important events were on the furniture horizon—a new line by Laverne and the Bertoia chairs by Knoll. The Laverne group, for which Lustig designed fabric and advertisements, created furniture that "reflects a clarity, grace and elegance that is unsurpassed in American furniture design." What he lauded was furniture that is consistent with his own interior design aesthetics, based on architectural traditions. He admired Harry Bertoia's chairs, an extension of the molded wire basket technique inaugurated by Charles Eames, and in his writing it was clear that he wanted to follow in that tradition, though he never had the chance.

EASTWARD HO

Lustig married Elaine Firstenberg in 1949, and by 1950 he wrote to James Laughlin that he was debating the pros and cons of returning to New York—siding with the pros. After his *Look* job, the first couple of years in Los Angeles gave him the opportunity "to try my wings at a lot of things I had not done before." However, he noted, "it has reached a point at which further development, especially financially is impossible."[80] So in January 1951, he and Elaine drove east for the last time. Lustig was invited to spend a month as adviser for the new design department at the University of Georgia in Athens, and he then ventured north to plant his final roots in New York. As their first home, on Mount Airy Road in Croton-on-Hudson, the couple rented a Lustron house, the pioneering prefab manufactured in response to the postwar housing shortage. Lustig, predictably, hated the bland cookie-cutter look of the metal exterior and did his best to disguise the interior by installing floor-to-ceiling drapes, his upholstered chair, some Eames chairs, typically airy cabinets and tables, and futuristic lighting. It was quite an ambitious effort for a one-year lease. The following year, he designed the Segal apartment, and a year later, his own apartment at 625 Park Avenue captured his focus; it was a project that continued until 1955.

Opposite top and bottom:
Alvin and Elaine outside the Lustron
house, 1952.

Above and bottom left:
Lustron house, 1951.
Living room.

Bottom right:
Lustig's Studebaker in the driveway
of the Lustron house, 1951.

Top:
William Segal private residence,
New York, 1952.
Dining room.

Bottom:
William Segal private residence,
New York, 1952.
Living room.

Opposite:
William Segal private residence,
New York, 1952.
Entrance.

Top:
Herta and Paul Wilheim private
residence apartment, New York 1955.
Living room.

Bottom:
Herta and Paul Wilheim private
residence apartment, New York 1955.
Study.

Opposite top:
Herta and Paul Wilheim private
residence apartment, New York 1955.
Dining room.

Opposite bottom:
Herta and Paul Wilheim private
residence apartment, New York 1955.
Cabinet and light fixtures.

One of Lustig's proudest accomplishments was the redesign of the first floor of the New York showrooms of Lightolier Inc. (11 East Thirty-sixth Street). He developed the space and color plan that was, according to Lightolier's public relations, "inviting, dramatic, and practical." Entering the showroom, the visitor was greeted by solid planes of bright, fresh color, anchored with black and white, while behind the reception desk was a highly decorative panel faced with white and gold rectangles. One side wall was fuchsia. The opposite wall, painted in matte black, included the Lightolier "crossed–L" brand, and in small white letters, the statement: "Wonderful things are happening in lighting!" Outside, light from the street sifted through a series of "thin-skin" panels set on tracks as a backdrop for the firm's display window. The Lightolier company was so pleased with Lustig's work that they dedicated a three-page press release detailing all the assets, concluding with: "The furniture in the reception area was specially designed by Lustig, and carries out the vital, clean-cut color plan evident elsewhere: Simple, angular seating pieces with white enameled metal frames are section-upholstered in solid mustard, flame, blue and black fabrics. A crowning element of festivity in light is a giant lighting fixture, also specially designed by Lustig: Three white metal hoops, each 45 inches in diameter and each carrying 48 tiny light bulbs, are looped one inside another and suspended from the high ceiling over the reception area."

Lustig's showroom, commercial interior, and exhibition designs are closely linked.

Arguably the Lightolier work influenced the scheme for his own retrospective exhibition. In 1949, he created a moveable, modular feast of his work for the A-D Gallery, in The Composing Room type house, which was directed by Dr. Robert Leslie. He was featured in other exhibits, including a wall of letters at the Museum of Modern Art's "Signs in the Street," curated in 1954 by Mildred Constantine, and "Two Graphic Designers: Alvin Lustig/Bruno Munari" (October 1955), but the A-D show, which traveled to the Walker Art Center's Everyday Art Gallery in 1950, was his own unique design.

Opposite:
Lustig's apartment, New York,
1953–55.
625 Park Avenue.
Dining area.

Top and bottom:
Lustig's apartment, New York,
1953–1955.
625 Park Avenue.
Living room.

Top and opposite:

Lustig exhibit at the Walker Art Center, 1950.

The Lustig exhibit originated at the A-D Gallery, The Composing Room, New York, in 1949 and traveled the next two years to various museums and galleries throughout the country. Lustig designed a special installation structure that held the panels of work. These stands were graduated in size so that they would nest inside one another and fit in one wooden shipping box. The drawing shows the panels, which were attached with clips.

Bottom:

Mural design for the Walker Art Center Lustig exhibit.

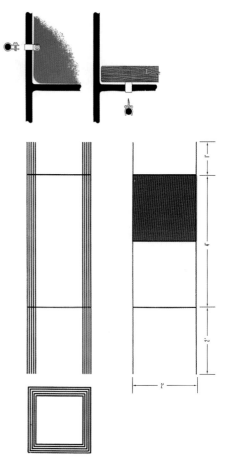

Leslie and his associate director, Hortense Mendel, were extremely enthusiastic about the exhibition ("it will do all of us proud," wrote Mendel in one of the dozens of lengthy letters to Lustig[81]). So they afforded him unprecedented license for design. In turn, Lustig made a spectacular display. He wrote detailed instructions for installation that made the complex assemblage foolproof—he hoped. "Assembling the exhibit is not difficult, but it does require that each step be taken in turn to avoid confusion," he wrote in a typically fastidious manner. The exhibition was modular, perfect for traveling. Transported in boxes, it contained five nesting steel stands, which stood seven feet tall; one group was painted black and the other white. These stands were the armature on which the frames and panels resided. "After all the frames and panels and models have been unwrapped," he continued, "the enclosed plan can be referred to for placement and the final task of assembling the loose material begun." Most of these components were given letter codes. Two types of

Above:

Signs in the Street, 1954.
Exhibition at the Museum of Modern Art, New York. Curated by Mildred Constantine. The black wall, 7¾' x 9½', had large, colored vacuum-formed plastic letters, including a Futura "b", a Gothic "E", a Gothic "A", a Clarendon "a", and a Severain "s". The letters were formed by Rohm & Haas.

Opposite top:
Catalog of the Lustig exhibition at the A-D Gallery, The Composing Room, 1948.

Opposite bottom:
Lustig exhibition invitation for the Frank Perls Gallery in Beverly Hills, which was the same exhibition as The Composing Room, 1950.

panels were designed, each with its own fastening device, either a screw clip or spring clip. The instructions continued for three single-spaced, typed pages, carefully guiding the installers from one frame to the next. Besides these materials, "you will find quite a few loose pieces consisting of books, book jackets and other items," he concluded. "These can be arranged on some of the empty walls indicated on the plan. You can use your own discretion as to arrangement. Chairs, plants, and a coffee table holding some of the books, and a case or table holding the rest of the books would help."[82] A sixteen-page catalog accompanied the show, about which Mendel wrote in a letter, "Bob and I are tremendously excited about it. I feel you have used very good judgment in the way you have balanced the various phases of your work. The whole [exhibition] presents a clean, uncluttered and simple exposition with a freshness that is very appealing."[83] After starting at the Walker Art Center (where a three-day symposium was held in Lustig's honor), the exhibit traveled

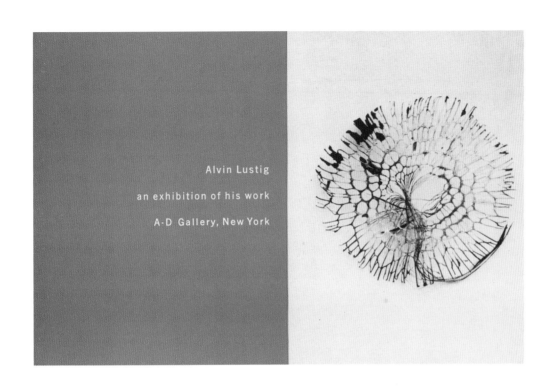

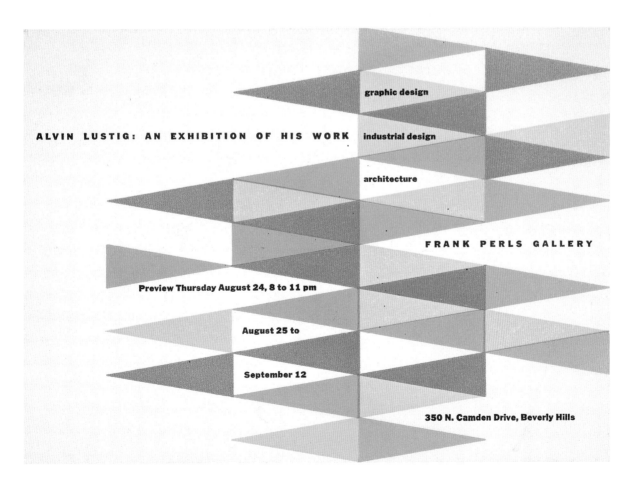

•

Top:

American Crayon exhibition, 1954.
Installed in a field at the Aspen Design
Conference.

Bottom:

Summer Trip, 1953.
Brochure for the American Crayon
Company.

•

Opposite:

Northland Shopping Center,
Detroit, 1954.
Complete design of signage: entrance
sign, parking lot signs, directional signs.
In collaboration with Victor Gruen and
Associates, Architects.

make creativeness part of your summer trip

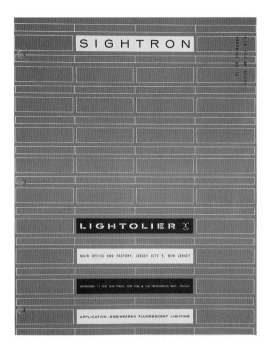

Top:
Lightolier, 1952.
One of a series of brochures
for its line of lighting products.

Bottom:
Lightolier, 1955
New Year's card.

Opposite:
Lightolier showroom, 1954.
Entrance, 11 East thirty-sixth Street,
New York.

to the Santa Barbara Museum, Frank Perls Gallery in Los
Angeles, Institute of Contemporary Arts in Washington,
D.C., and Skidmore College in Saratoga Springs, New York.
Other institutions and schools were also clamoring for a
chance to show it.

In 1955, Lustig was included in one of MoMA's "What Is Good
Design?" shows, which underscored his growing reputation.
But the dual showing at MoMA with Italian designer Bruno
Munari, from October 18 to November 27, 1955, just a few
weeks before his death, was the zenith of his career. Although
Lustig did not design the installation, it was a huge honor to
be showcased in the hallowed halls of Modernism. One of the
wall captions noted: "Lustig's preoccupation with formal
elements of design, combined with his ability to subordinate
whatever is irrelevant to his purpose, gives his work its consistent distinction."

Lustig's last few months were taken up with the exhibition
and a number of commissions. In an undated letter to a friend
he wrote, "to be rather blunt I have not been able to see at
all since the first of October. Starting around the end of
June . . . the good left eye began to grow foggy and daily
grew dimmer until now I can only distinguish dark from
light . . . Only one or two people were aware of the situation
and I was doing some rather fancy faking to carry on."[84]
Ultimately, he told people the truth and, blind or not, he
continued to work on his commissions. "My work has always
been visualized in the minds [*sic*] eye and you probably
remember how little sketching or drawing I did."[85] And so he
continued to work. "Actually there has been no diminution in
the quantity or range of work we are doing," he wrote in a
November 1954 letter to his friend William De Mayo in London. "One of the things that heartened me is that we're just
negotiating the contract with Loft's Candies, one of the large
eastern chain stores, to do four stores for them on an experimental basis." Loft's had just accepted the first design,
including changes in their basic typography and trademark.
"This added to other recent encouraging events has made it
easier for me to go on, although I will not deny I've had my
moments of despair."[86]

TEACHING MODERN
Designer as Educator

"Teaching is a lot of fun, although it takes a great deal out of one."

This inadvertent rhyme by Alvin Lustig in one of his frequent letters to James Laughlin (c. 1946) lacks the gravitas of his academic writing but is indicative of Lustig's sense of play. His serious side was often cut with wit, and his studious side was sometimes underpinned by mischievousness. In the same paragraph—in fact, the next sentence—he cut to: "My love life is as usual non-existent . . . The fires are dying." Nonetheless from all accounts, though romance was on the wane, he was getting all fired up over design education.

By the mid-'40s, Lustig took every opportunity to augment his design practice with teaching and lecturing. In the late '40s, he spoke frequently to high school art teachers in Los Angeles; in 1950, he addressed fine- and commercial-art classes at Pasadena City College. "The faculty members have long looked upon you as one of the foremost designers in advertising and industrial design," wrote Helen Reid, chair of the art department. "It will, therefore, be a pleasure for us to hear you speak on contemporary design, and it will be an especial treat to our students who look forward ultimately to qualify for work in related fields."[87]

Lustig relished spreading his gospel. "I have discovered what a great number of people already realize—the apparent inability, so far, for education to produce people who are capable of finding some reasonable specialized activity that will give them a 'hook' onto the existing economic situation and, at the same time, produce people even though they are involved in a technical society. The technical students from the art schools usually get trapped into some form of 'hackdom'— either a low-paid hackdom or a high-paid hackdom, but still hackdom. The college students in most cases wander into any number of activities."[88] He sought, whenever possible, to wed theory and practice into what, at the time, was a new wave of pedagogy—design as art rather than as trade.

The first chance to test his theories was in 1945, when the former Bauhaus master Josef Albers asked him to develop a course for the Black Mountain College Summer Institute in rural North Carolina. Founded in 1933 by John A. Rice and Theodore Dreier, Black Mountain was a unique experiment that integrated art studies as a central component of liberal arts education. The progressive nature of the college attracted such avant-garde faculty as Buckminster Fuller, John Cage, Ben Shahn, and Robert Motherwell. A few members of the defunct Bauhaus, which had been closed by the Nazis, including Walter Gropius, Xanti Schawinsky, and Anni Albers, also taught there.

design

april, 1946 / vol. 47   no. 8 / 35c

special issue: black
mountain
college

architecture   painting
design   sculpture
photography   graphic design
weaving

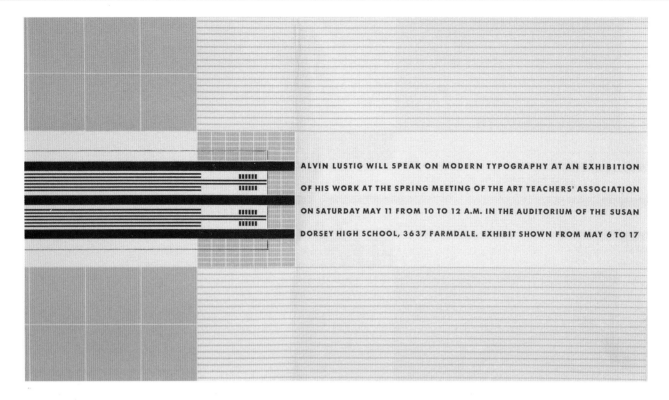

ALVIN LUSTIG WILL SPEAK ON MODERN TYPOGRAPHY AT AN EXHIBITION OF HIS WORK AT THE SPRING MEETING OF THE ART TEACHERS' ASSOCIATION ON SATURDAY MAY 11 FROM 10 TO 12 A.M. IN THE AUDITORIUM OF THE SUSAN DORSEY HIGH SCHOOL, 3637 FARMDALE. EXHIBIT SHOWN FROM MAY 6 TO 17

Lustig's theories of teaching and practice of design were essentially the same. "It is the job of the designer to deal creatively with the ever-present conflict between tradition and new technology," wrote R. Holland Melson in "Alvin Lustig: the Designer as Teacher."[89] Lustig believed that, like architecture, graphic design was an industrial process that demanded complete mastery of all the technical processes. And yet, he felt that there was need for a new course of study—more on the model of the Bauhaus—different from the common trade school program that equipped students with skills, yet failed to give them the tools to deal with ideas. He sought to invest students with critical ability. "His aim," added Melson, paraphrasing his former teacher, "was to produce creative people capable of competing in a technical society." Lustig once said—as many have subsequently argued—"I don't believe that you can teach creative art. I think all you can teach is a certain awareness, and open a number of doors. I don't really believe in art education; that's the reason I'm willing to try it out in various ways."[90] He did, however, view school as a hothouse for research and development outside the purview of the work-a-day world.

Albers knew instinctively that Lustig would complement his Black Mountain coursework, rooted in the Bauhaus aesthetic.

For his part, Lustig viewed Albers's invitation as an incredible opportunity to build a unique pedagogy. He wrote about his brief tenure: ". . . the course began by demonstrating its relationship to the basic design classes of Albers, and attempted to show methods of extending and developing these discoveries into the graphic field. The intricacies of typography, engraving and printing processes were discussed, hastily however, because of the shortness of the course. This was followed by an explanation of 'approach' to the graphic problem and the psychological factors involved in 'selling' not only the public but the man who is paying for the work. The pitfalls and dangers, both personal and external, that make good work in this field still rare were pointed out. The class worked on a few minor problems to develop a certain amount of technical proficiency, and then spent the bulk of the time solving a specific problem which involved all that had been discussed."[91]

The ordinarily brusque Albers was indeed pleased with the outcome, and said so. "Many thanks again for your coming to us and for your very helpful and successful course," he wrote to Lustig. "The more I think it over the more I believe that we should continue such work here. I hope you are able to come again."[92]

Lustig was pleased with the opportunity to teach more. "The emotional atmosphere is, to put it mildly, supercharged," he wrote to Laughlin. "The second day here, two girls told me they loved me . . . Am apparently quite a success as a teacher. Have a large enthusiastic class. Lots of interesting people here, and altogether having a very stimulating time. Music, lectures, classes and parties follow each other in a vicious and endless circle."[93] His stay was, he also wrote, occasionally disrupted by female entanglements, which he insisted he tried to avoid. "The last week has been blissfully uncomplicated by the opposite sex," he wrote in a so-called biweekly report to Laughlin. "Have been carefully arranging it so that I am never with anyone except a faculty member, and then no one under forty." His social set nonetheless increased exponentially, with a continuous flow of faculty and guest lecturers.

"My relationship to teaching has only recently been established, and has been very minor," he wrote in the *Western Arts Association Bulletin*, "so I feel perhaps the greatest contribution I can make is to take the place of the interloper or 'thorn in the side' and compare teaching experience with outside experience, and attempt to relate some of the ideas that we teach to the general pattern of our existence."[94]

Lustig ultimately felt that teaching was integral to the next stage of his career. He wrote about having "a naïve faith that somehow the school is the area in which a kind of experimentation and research, not possible in the work-a-day world, is taking place." But he also warned, "when the work-a-day world, however, outstrips the school in theoretical as well as practical knowledge, something is seriously wrong. This is a situation that has not yet been resolved in the entire education process." And this problem in search of a solution is what caused him to decide "that perhaps I should explore teaching a bit."[95] So in 1946 he accepted a two-day-a-week appointment at Art Center School, then on West Third Street in Los Angeles, teaching an advanced graphic and industrial design class. In addition to the pedagogy, he enjoyed the regular salary. "They are paying me quite well so that I will be able to choose only work that really interests me," he wrote to Laughlin.[96] For its part, Art Center thought enough of

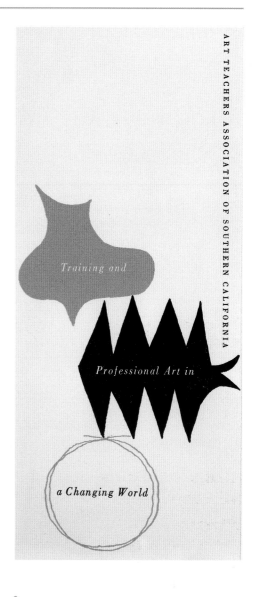

Page 176:
Alvin Lustig at Art Center, 1948.

Page 179:
Design, A Special Issue, Black Mountain College, 1946.
Magazine cover. The issue also included an article by Lustig.

Opposite:
Art Teachers Association of Southern California, early 1940s.
Invitation to a lecture by Lustig and an exhibtion of his work. Most probably his first exhibition.

Above:
Art Teachers Association of Southern California, 1947.
Meeting at Art Center School to discuss "Training and Professional Art in a Changing World."

top-flight designers join our staff!

GEORGE JERGENSON
11 years with the General Motors Styling Section. Principal designer of the Train of Tomorrow and head of Product Design Department. Contributed to the styling of Buick. Chief Designer of Cadillac.

ALVIN LUSTIG
Brilliant stylist of modern stores, shops and specialized structures. Noted graphic designer, formerly director of design for Look magazine. Designer for Fortune, "New Direction" and Knopf publications.

JOHN DEE COLEMAN
Former Director of Design for Aviation Corp. Responsible for post-war styling of planes, power tools, refrigerators and appliances. Has contributed to the design of both General Motors and Hudson cars.

A. ALBERT COOLING
Modern Designer. Prizes include: House & Garden's post-war homes, Progressive Architecture's G.I. home competitions, Grand prize, "Colotyle" bathroom competition; Libby-Owens-Ford competition.

THE ART CENTER SCHOOL proudly announces the addition of 4 distinguished designers to its staff of 43. With these and other specialists, Art Center Industrial students undergo intensive training in Package and Display, Merchandising, Transportation, Product Design and other Specialized Structures. Design principles are approached experimentally, include three-dimensional projects and lead to complete scale models and finished products. Complete analyses. market requirements and manufacturing methods are integrated with training in drafting, model-making and rendering. Clinical evaluations by outside specialists are held periodically. Motion Picture Set Design, Photography and the Graphic Arts are related subjects in the School. The design approach and teaching methods employed by the School have gained for 17 years nation-wide recognition by both the Profession and Industry. *For further details, write to the Industrial Design Registrar. New term begins May 24.*

THE ART CENTER SCHOOL

5353 W. 3rd Street, Los Angeles 5, California

Edward A. Adams, *Director*

A Non-Profit Institution – Now in Its Seventeenth Year

Above:

"4 Top-Flight Designers Join Our Staff!" 1948.
Advertisement for The Art Center School
published in *Arts & Architecture*.

Opposite:

"Three Important Days in May," 1947.
Invitation for Art Teachers Association
of Southern California.

Lustig to include him in a magazine advertisement "proudly" announcing "4 Top-Flight Designers Join Our Staff!"

Lustig's impact was equally significant. "Alvin was a breath of fresh air and the whole class worshiped him," said Eugene Weston, an architect and former student.[97] "Some of us were lucky enough to work for him at the Sunset Street office," where Weston created working drawings for Lustig on a spec house he designed but was never built.

Despite Lustig's favorable impression, he was disappointed in Art Center and left after less than two years. "My first teaching was in a private art school which puts emphasis on graphic and industrial design," he wrote in the *Western Arts Association Bulletin*. "It is without doubt one of the best in the country from a technical standpoint. It produces people of great manual facility. . . . It had the trade school's strength and the trade school's failure; the ability to produce highly specialized technicians—but the inability to produce people related in understanding to a larger social community or human endeavor."[98]

In 1948, a core group of Lustig's students left Art Center in a protest over E. A. Adams, who was appointed to head the industrial design department, and whose curriculum was not considered to be very challenging. "I was just a kid out of high school," explained Peter Dodge, an architect who studied with and later worked for Lustig, "but my very serious WW II veteran friends thought the course too lightweight, so they left and I left with them."[99] They went to another institution, the California School of Art on Hoover Street in central Los Angeles, where Lustig began teaching in 1948 along with Edgardo Contini, Rafael Soriano, and Edgardo Tacket. The school lasted only one year, since its shady owner absconded to Mexico with the school's funds. The most prominent of Lustig's students were John Follis and Rex Goode, who later started *Architectural Pottery*, and Louis Danziger.

In 1950, Lustig moved on to the University of Southern California, where he taught two classes in the fine arts department. This assignment lasted only one semester. About the

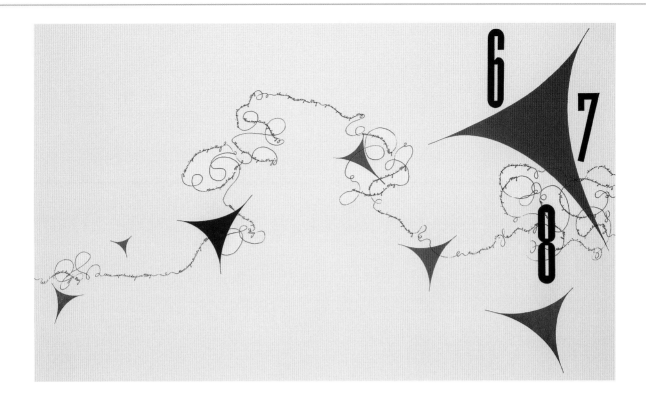

experience he wrote: "The next opportunity to teach was at a university in the same area, where just exactly the opposite situation existed. Here I found people who talked quite cleverly about almost everything and with highly developed critical faculties, but who couldn't do a thing."[100]

This schism between theory and practice, thinking and doing—a common complaint among educators and practitioners—was at the root of a crisis in contemporary design education. So it was fortuitous that in 1950 Lamar Dodd, head of the Department of Art at the University of Georgia, invited Lustig for a four-week stint to consult on the creation of an industrial design department. Lustig proposed that a strong design program be closely related to painting programs. "It is the painter, dealing in private symbols, who is involved in pure research, while it is the designer's task to draw freely upon this research in the creation of public symbols," wrote Melson about Lustig's concept.[101] Another of Lustig's initial proposals was to make a darkroom available to students, not to produce professional photographers, but to make the essential tool of photography available.

Lustig wrote a brief proposal for Dodd that served as the foundation for Lustig's future educational concepts:

SCOPE OF THE PROGRAM:

Facing the lack of a basic architectural course or technical facility, what sort of program could the university build on its existing foundations which would still have a maximum potential for integration with the industrial and general community?

The University of Georgia could make up for its lack of technical facilities by producing students of superior ability and understanding, the new "design integrators" who are able to unify all aspects of a problem, technical, economic and psychological. Increasingly, each of these functions must be fulfilled by a specialist, but the designer must create a whole of these parts. The school could not practically enter into actual product design instruction, but by the nature of its training, students could be produced who would have a wide enough understanding of general design principles that they could fit well into such specialized needs, with some additional experience.

Lustig was ahead of other educators, though consistent with Bauhaus teaching when he noted, "one can envisage a program where business and industry not only seek for trained design help from the student body of the university, but where the

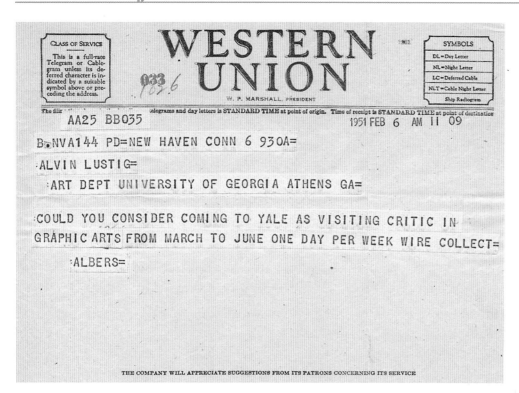

university itself, working with both faculty and students, could provide advisory and research facilities which could not be duplicated by the industries themselves."[102]

He insisted that the training and education would be entirely different from the usual concept of an art department. "Design is a very different kind of activity from painting, sculpture, or crafts, even though there are points of contact between these areas," he wrote. "There is a slight tendency at the University of Georgia to consider design as an inferior activity to the so-called 'fine arts,' indulged in by those without sufficient talent to be painters or sculptors. I have no intention of discussing a hierarchy of creative values in this paper, but I do wish to point out that all successful design schools, both here and abroad, have never shared this attitude." He made a note about those design schools with creative painters on their faculty. "It is interesting to note that Paul Klee at the Bauhaus once taught the metal shop class, designing such objects as door knobs and the like."[103]

A viable design major, he suggested, should not be part of the fine arts department—a radical concept—but instead should be run by an "autonomous head" of the design department. "The function of this overall design chairman, which should include instruction in one of the classes, would be that

of establishing the main lines of the program, maintaining its integrity and relation to the community at large. This person, besides possessing unquestioned design ability, should have administrative and community-relations talents. His task would be one of contacting and winning over those members of the larger community who could both help and be helped by such a program." Lustig also insisted that he have a wide reach within the profession of design, in order to bring in visiting critics and advisers of real ability. "The last phase of his rather herculean task would be to project the vitality of such a program widely enough that it would not only attract the best caliber students in the South but would bring them down from the North as well."[104]

As for the faculty, Lustig argued that design instructors, "to be at all valid, must have had some reasonable personal success in the field in which they propose to teach. Most graduates of teachers' colleges with design teaching backgrounds, but with no actual experience in the field, are worse than useless." But attracting such teachers would not be easy unless the salaries were sufficiently high.

All students would be required to take basic art courses: life drawing, perspective and rudimentary drafting, lettering, basic design both two- and three-dimensional, and a contemporary art and architecture orientation course that would be separate from an art history course. He determined that at that time the university's basic design class was not adequate. "The design difficulties that develop later in the more specialized classes, such as graphic and interior design, reflect the inadequacies of the basic design and orientation classes."[105]

He also maintained that crafts should not be considered as part of the design course, although the opportunity for some experience in this field should be available to the designers. "Crafts should either be an independent department or should be a branch of the 'fine arts' department," he wrote. "Crafts provide a humanizing, laboratory experience for the designer which is very useful but which is quite often over-emphasized."[106]

Lustig focused on the graphic and interior design programs as ripe for improvement. It was necessary to have good typographic equipment—typefaces, proof presses, and printing equipment should be available. Every effort should be made to make this department "the design control center for every piece of graphic design coming out of the university." Such a program, he believed, if properly guided, could within a period of five years make itself felt with considerable vigor. "It would require a rare combination of skill, tact, intelligence, energy and additional funds but enough of those ingredients are already present to make it seem quite within the realm of possibility."

Josef Albers had heard about Lustig's foray into program development and, on February 6, 1951, sent him a telegram (left) with the following request: "Could you consider coming to Yale as visiting critic in graphic arts from March to June one day per week—Albers." Six months earlier, Albers had been named the chairman of a new Department of Design at Yale. The department offered a four-year course with a revised professional curriculum in painting, sculpture, and the graphic arts leading to a bachelor of fine arts degree and was closely affiliated with the Departments of Architecture and Drama. Lustig responded in the affirmative, but with a stipulation: He preferred not to work with undergraduates.

Top:
Alvin Lustig critiquing an exhibition model in an industrial design class at the Art Center School, Los Angeles, circa 1949. Photo © Art Center College of Design.

Bottom:
Alvin and Elaine with Richard Neutra at the 1954 Aspen Design Conference.

Lustig at Yale University, 1952.

"As to your preference to deal with advanced students, [Alvin] Eisenman thinks it could be arranged," wrote Albers on February 23, 1951. He added by way of caveat, "As most of the students are majoring in painting—I encourage the painters to learn lettering and typography—they are inclined to think first of etching, lithography, etc. Just recently we were able to introduce class problems with emphasis on typographic problems."

Lustig ended up doing more than fulfilling the duties of a visiting critic (a position that still exists at Yale today), which was his official title. He also developed the "Experimental Workshop in Graphic Design." He wrote a detailed description, a synthesis of all his previous ideas that addressed the following aims (reproduced in full):

EXPERIMENTAL WORKSHOP IN GRAPHIC DESIGN FOR YALE UNIVERSITY

Aims: The experimental workshop in graphic design would have the following general aims:

• To help provide criteria and guidance for the establishment of standards in the field of graphic design. This is to be done by publication of periodicals, books, exhibitions, seminars, and international exchange with designers in other countries.

• To establish a working relationship and interchange of ideas between the graphic design profession and a more experimental unhampered laboratory. It would provide an opportunity for proven practitioners in the field to work on projects of a sort which the usual pressure of their business would not allow. Outside industry would present problems of a graphic design nature that the center would attempt to solve.

• To make available to students in the graphic design department stimulating contacts with the active graphic design profession, in order to smooth the gap between school and practical work. This would be achieved by their helping in both a research and creative capacity, projects that would be developed within the center or would be suggested by an outside advisory board.

• To gather together in one place type specimens, periodicals, graphic collections, and other information related to graphic design, and to provide a center where all people engaged in the profession might go for information and reference material.

Organization: The workshop would be under the co-direction of the School of Design of Yale University and the Museum of Modern Art. Yale University would provide the main creative and productive impetus with its present staff and facilities, although the workshop would be organized separately from the present graphic design curriculum. The Museum of Modern Art would provide critical guidance, space for exhibitions and seminars, help in gathering reference material, and personnel for these activities would be as follows:

• Yale University: Josef Albers, Alvin Lustig (director), Alvin Eisenman, Herbert Matter.

• Museum of Modern Art: Philip G. Johnson, Arthur Drexler, Mildred Constantine (director), and staff.

• An advisory board consisting of influential and creative people would meet at intervals to make suggestions as to the direction, possible problems, and general advice concerning the conduct of the workshop. They would also help in suggesting the sources of funds to underwrite the activity of the workshop. This group would be selected as individuals and would not represent the firms or institutions which employed them. The following is a tentative list for such a group:

> • Consulting Advisory Board to include: Charles Coiner, Leo Lionni, Bill Golden, Charles Eames, Robert Osborn, Walter Howe, Bradbury Thompson, Alexey Brodovitch.

> • Aside from this group, a less official group of foreign designers such as [Willem] Sandberg (Holland), Max Bill (Switzerland), Otl Aicher (Germany), and Bruno Munari (Italy) would help to keep the center informed of international happenings.

Program: Initial program suggestions that could be undertaken with the present staff are:

• Development and publication of a basic text book on contemporary typography.

• Students assigned to develop ideas related to it.

• Students assigned to research on existing books and articles relating to contemporary typography.

• Writing, planning and designing books.

• Probable publication by Yale University Press.

• Development of new typefaces.

• Seeking out little known foreign and domestic type faces for purchase and inclusion in the Yale collection.

• Work with architects to improve and develop public lettering: street signs, building plaques, etc.

• Work with TV people on titles, animation, backdrop material for advertising.

• New presentation of established media for night advertising.

• General experiment with advertising and book typography.

• Development of a periodical to be issued by the workshop dealing with problems of graphic design.

• Development of small exhibitions based on drawings and photographs of Victorian public lettering found on old buildings on the Eastern seaboard.

• Design guidance in the preparation of a periodical to be published by the architectural department.

• Accumulation of type specimens from all available type foundries both here and abroad.

Budget: Every effort would be made to keep the initial expenditure at a minimum. The present staff facilities would be sufficient for a good beginning. However, additional funds would be needed for adequate growth and such funds would have to be raised by gifts from interested individuals, firms or foundations. The following are some of the expenses which would be covered by such funds:

• Overhead: Secretarial assistance part time; announcements; letterheads.

• Equipment: Increase in supplies already in use at Yale and purchase of books and periodicals relative to the field.

• Fellowships: To students and professionals; increase in staff.

Lustig continued to work with Yale, making the weekly trek to New Haven from 1951 to 1953. The master educational concepts the program adhered to, as well as the Bauhaus sensibility that prevailed, derived primarily from Lustig's basic plan. He left the school when his deteriorating vision made it too difficult to continue. But even out of the classroom he never lost his fervent passion for teaching.

MESSIANIC MODERN
Designer as Author

In 1954, Alvin Lustig gave a lecture titled "What Is a Designer?" at the Advertising Typographers Association of America. It was one of many such talks he gave to organizations, art directors' clubs, and schools around the United States and Canada. However, this lecture was different. It was his first speech after he lost his eyesight. Yet there he stood, firmly planted on the stage, fervently spreading his gospel about the importance of good design to the world at large. Another person might have declined the invitation to speak after such a medical trauma, but Lustig was so committed to his message he couldn't—and wouldn't—miss the opportunity.

Lustig had a curious religious side; in fact, for a brief time in his youth he embraced Jesus and the idea of messiah, but just as quickly returned to being a cultural Jew. He possessed "a sense of order in the universe," wrote Arthur A. Cohen, which fostered the belief that design was an essential means of making Earth a better place. Since this conference was possibly one of Lustig's last chances to take the bully pulpit, "What Is a Designer?" had an even more strident tone than earlier talks. He implored his audience to action. Addressing advertising art directors, who with few exceptions prior to the mid-'50s' "Creative Revolution" did not hold truly influential positions, he urged them not to succumb to conventions but to become "designers with a capital D." This Modernist, holistic notion, born at the Bauhaus and other progressive academies, lay dormant with few exceptions for decades until the late twentieth century, when the so-called citizen designer emerged. Lustig's fervency was ahead of the curve in the early '50s.

One way to impact the world, if only in a small way, was to propagate design through writing. Lustig exhorted listeners and readers to view the commonplace in uncommon ways: In "What Is a Designer?" he explained, "design is related in some way to the world, the society that creates it. Whether you're talking about architecture, furniture, clothing, homes, public buildings, utensils, equipment, each period of design is an expression of society, people will respond most warmly and directly to those designs which express their feelings and their tastes." In just a few sentences, he clarified the responsibility of designers and the purpose of design, characterizing it as a noble yet profoundly misunderstood art and craft.

In his writing for trade magazines and journals, including the *AIGA Journal*, *Design Quarterly*, *Publishers Weekly*, *Interiors*, and the newsletter *Type Talks*, utopian optimism was central to Lustig's aims to raise the standards of design, especially graphic design. His prose, while formal and sometimes too wordy, is at once reasoned and critical. Nonetheless, he did not pull punches when the need arose, a trait that was uncommon in the overly polite design community.

In 1958, some of Lustig's better texts were anthologized in *The Collected Writings of Alvin Lustig*, edited by Holland R. Melson and funded with a grant given to the Yale art department by Elaine Lustig. This small, limited-edition volume is the only collection of Lustig's talks and essays ever published, although a few pieces have been published in larger anthologies. Through these essays, it is possible to "hear" Lustig's thought process, although no recordings of him exist.

When Lustig started seriously writing about design in the late 1940s, only a few American designers were practicing basic journalism, while scholarly and professional criticism were virtually absent, although there were copious amounts of both in Europe. The most prolific among the American writers was the typographer and book designer William Addison Dwiggins, who coined the term "graphic designer" in an article titled "A New Kind of Printing Calls for New Design" in *The Boston Evening Transcript* in 1922. Industrial designers like Norman Bel Geddes and Walter Dorwin Teague were prolific, and both wrote career-defining books (the former's 1940 *Magic Motorways* suggests prescient guidelines for a new American infrastructure, and the latter's 1940 *Design This Day* encouraged a nation emerging battered from the Depression to tap into design for strength and power). On the graphic design side, fewer designers were publishing. Paul Rand was an exception with *Thoughts on Design*, published by Wittenborn in 1947 (although it would be almost four decades until he published another book). A few professional "design writers" reported in professional journals or trade magazines such as *Advertising Arts*, *American Printer*, *PM/AD*, and *Print* (and briefly in the lavish, short-lived *Portfolio*). These venues for "trade journalism," however, lacked the rigor of art, literary, or architecture criticism. Of course, there was never an accepted vocabulary for graphic or industrial design criticism, so the language was ad hoc. Thus, it was something of an occasion when Lustig wrote about graphic design as a crucial discipline for practice and scholarship.

In his essay titled "Graphic Design" in the short-lived *Design* magazine, Lustig explained a rationale behind conceiving the graphic design program at the Black Mountain Summer Institute. The essay became something of a manifesto for his pedagogy. He emphasized "the fact that graphic design is slowly emerging as a serious art on its own terms."[107] While this was implicit in essays and manifestos issued during the '20s and '30s by members of the European avant-garde, it was rarely discussed in the United States. Today Lustig's words are as familiar as they were then unexpected—and they have become something of an anthem for contemporary design writers. "The basic difference between the graphic designer and the painter or sculptor," he wrote, "is his search for the 'public' rather than the 'private' symbol. His aim is to clarify and open the channels of communication rather than limit or even obscure them, which is too often the preoccupation of those only dealing with the personal symbol." While he was warning designers away from self-indulgence, he also acknowledged parity between graphic and other design forms and their industrial ties. "Graphic design, like architecture, is an industrial process and demands complete mastery of all the technical conditions, as the designer depends entirely on a set of skilled workmen he has never met to carry out his plans."

Lustig's essays regarding pedagogy are as valuable for what they reveal about the early stages of progressive design education as they are for illuminating his own role in the process. In "Designing, A Process of Teaching," Lustig proffered design as its own art form. "I have a great interest in painting because I think painting at this moment still carries the superior vitality," he wrote. "Certainly the painter is doing a kind of research that the designer can't do," but he added that painting has its limitations, and that design, which is a more public than private activity, is becoming a venue for progressive expression. "These great private symbols which [painters] have evolved are now waiting to be projected onto the public level, and the painter confronted by these gigantic gestures, is almost powerless." In adhering to the Modern *gesamtkunstwerk* (total work of art) principle, Lustig was a proponent of the idea that art for art's sake and art for function's sake could be one and the same.

Here he admitted that rather than maintain carefully worked theories of design, "I would reverse the process and try to track down the instinctive, the quite often unconscious development which leads one later to feel that such a theory is necessary." In one of his most eloquent essays on the process of design—a keen example of critical analysis—he wrote: "I have found that all positions men take in their beliefs are profoundly influenced by thousands of small, often imperceptible experiences that slowly accumulate to form a sum total of choices and decisions." In fact, this essay is an explanation of how he became a "modern" rather than a "traditional" designer. He continued: "I hope the reader will forgive me if this becomes personal, but tracing this kind of organic development is very vital." And he went on to discuss the ability to "'see' freshly, unencumbered by preconceived verbal, literary or moral ideas . . . The inability to respond directly to the vitality of forms is a curious phenomenon and one that people of our country suffer from to a surprising degree."[108]

Lustig's designs fluidly shift from past to present. For his early "experimental" work he built upon an armature of old technologies (metal type) and techniques (neo-constructivism), which evolved through new technologies (photographic manipulations) into unprecedented styles (his own interpretation of the Modern). Toward the end of his life, his typography turned into a playful amalgam of vintage letters composed in contemporary layouts with vibrant colors. In "Personal Notes," he wrote, "As we become more mature we will learn to master the interplay between past and present and not be so self-conscious of our rejection or acceptance of tradition. We will not make the mistake that both rigid modernists and conservatives make, of confusing the quality of form with the specific forms themselves."

He was also concerned with the state of Modernism in the design world and weary of the traditionalist versus Modernist wars—while at the same time he was a staunch supporter of the Modern ethos. "Like all revolutionaries the modern designers have always been a little self-conscious and even defensive," he wrote in notes for an unpublished essay on

the virtues of modern printing. "Now that the battle shows signs of having been won it is time to reexamine the situation. As is always the case with revolutions, some have reversed themselves completely. A man like [Jan] Tschichold, after evolving some of the basic tenets of modern typography, has decided that he is all wrong and has reverted to a kind of static conservatism that even outdoes the traditionalists. We will not go into the psychology of the turn-coat, but it is sufficient to say that the mentality that is capable of this kind of action certainly is not an example of the deeply felt inner necessity . . . It is a peculiarly European performance and is a direct outgrowth of the manifesto-spawning characteristics of their art activities. It is inconceivable that a personality like Frank Lloyd Wright would suddenly announce that he had been all wrong and henceforth he will build only in the classic style."[109] He often used simple themes like "what is modern printing?" to expound on larger design issues.

The more Lustig engaged in various disciplines in his studio, the more he wrote about subjects other than graphic design. Architecture was a significant theme, and despite his lack of architectural vocabulary, he was articulate on the subject. Various drafts of published articles and unpublished notes in his archive give voice to his interest in, and at times frustration with, contemporary architectural practice. In a short essay (perhaps notes for a lecture), he wrote about dichotomies that troubled him (and have in recent years risen to the surface of design consciousness): "Another strong line of division which has been too arbitrary has been the choice between purely esthetic gestures which pretend to ignore social consequences and architecture whose claim to worth has been based primarily on certain social attitudes ignoring a certain degree [of] refinement of design." And in a similar text he argued on the side of modern American architecture having its own spirit: "America is a growing synthesis of extremely varied ethnic, political and religious strains and so will be her architecture . . . No less an American than Louis Sullivan in a lecture given in 1897 said that the destiny of American architecture will be to merge the apparently conflicting architectures of heart and mind, a fusion he pointed to that has not yet taken place in the history of man." He was adamant in his own work, as well as his more general worldview that "America can still learn the lessons and discipline of intellectual rigor from Europe without fear of tainting or losing her on own vital character."[110]

Ultimately, Lustig's interest in architecture underpinned both his practice and theory of typography. In raw notes for yet another lecture, he resolutely sought to address "the relationship of the organizing principles of letterforms and organizing principles of architecture . . . [and] show those examples in which the letter and the building are conceived in the same terms of construction and those in which the letters have a life of their own and grow from principles quite independent of architecture."[111] The graphic design and architecture nexus was eventually embraced by younger designers, in large part thanks to Lustig's writing.

In May 1955, just six months before he died, Lustig submitted to Harry Ford, an editor at Alfred A. Knopf, a proposal for a monograph. "Enclosed is the précis for a book," he wrote. "I've tried, as you suggested, to make it rather detailed and specific although I found I didn't have to much to [sic] say." (See appendix 2.) This last line is rather ironic given both the length of the précis and the depth of the proposal he sent to Ford on July 8. His thematic chapters/essays were decidedly progressive for American design but consistent with European concepts. They include "The Designer In a Living Society," "Structure and the Sense of Order," "Private and Public Symbols," "Design Education," "Scale and Environment," "Principles of Contemporary Typography," and "An Approach to Architectural Lettering." (See appendix 3.) Subsequent correspondence with Ford and Sidney Jacobs, Knopf's production manager, reveal that there was serious interest in doing the book. Lustig provided a "breakdown of the physical content [that] has been worked out rather carefully in relationship to the specific material and I think presents a fairly accurate picture." After detailing his desires, Lustig noted: "This is about as specific as I can be without sitting down and actually designing the book. If we can come reasonably close to this

general character I would be very pleased." The intricate production specs Lustig proposed met with the following response from Jacobs: "I am completely confounded by the mathematics of your précis for the book you propose to do." Discussion about the project did not go further.

The untitled monograph was never published; so we will never know how significant the book might have been in the world of design. By 1955, Lustig was garnering a sizable amount of press (both in the trade and mainstream periodicals), so interest in a monograph was potentially high. The outline indicates that the themes elevate design and design writing to a higher level than existed at the time. The fact that the book was, in its formative stage, not solely celebrating Lustig's achievements but also promoting good design, may have afforded this a much wider readership than typical design books.

Page 188:
Alvin Lustig, 1944.
Photograph by Maya Deren.

Page 194:
Magnolia from *27 Wagons*
book jacket.

Epilogue

In the decades since Alvin Lustig died, design has evolved as practice and art in ways he would have liked, particularly as a force for change. The rediscovery of Lustig by the design world also proves that the kind of holistic thinking he proffered back in the '40s and '50s is indeed current today. That Lustig was forgotten until recently, except by those who knew him, is due to the lack of a codified design history and the myopia of younger designers who look forward, not backward, until they are older and wiser. With the onslaught of graphic design history books, classes, exhibitions, and conferences since the mid-1980s, Lustig's major contributions have been justly resurrected, not simply as manifestations of a late Modern style (although they are), but for what his work and ideas say about the role of the iconoclast—the individual designer—in the larger popular culture. He once wrote that it was not the role of the designer to express personal ego but rather to seek "through reason to erect his economic role." He meant that designers should be responsible for producing necessary manufactures and goods that "have meaning and beauty." Lustig's work, as presented in this volume, is not nostalgic but is a still viable foundation, or at least solid building blocks, for contemporary practice. His graphic design may not be as revelatory as it was when first introduced, but it still appears fresh even in this digital, overly ornamented world. Yet most important, his fundamental philosophy, that design is a total practice, integrated and interdependent, that gives both pleasure and purpose to society and culture, is the underlying rationale for much of the practice today. In this sense, Lustig laid the foundation for what designers do today. His touch of genius has blossomed into total genius.

ROSE

APPENDIX 1
IN MEMORIAM: ALVIN LUSTIG

By James Laughlin, 1955

Among the poems of Greek Anthology there is one whose author is listed as "Parrhasios, the Painter." I do not know who Parrhasios was but I think that the poem he left us might also have been written by our friend Alvin Lustig.

"And this I say . . . that my hand has fixed the limit of this art.
And (though no mortal work can exist without flaw)
This my mark is established for ever and will not Be passed."

The world will remember Alvin for the unique creations of his hand and eye, but we his friends, who are gathered here together to wish him farewell, will remember him because he was a clear light in a darkening world, because he was a man who had his vision and saw his path and followed them without deviation, because he was a gentle heart who never raised his hand or his voice, because he was a warm but tactful friend who gave of himself to us so readily and so easily that few of us ever stopped to measure the gift.

I first met Alvin nearly twenty years ago. A friend took me to the studio in Brentwood, near Los Angeles, where Alvin had set up a small hand press to work out his experiments in typographic design. I had only to be with him an hour to realize that I had come to know an authentic creative genius. His graphic work was just beginning but already it was unique. Alvin opened my eyes to what a book could be, just as later he was to show others how a room could be more than they had imagined, or how an office could be as beautiful as a work of art. But what I think of most when I go back in my mind over twenty years of friendship and work together is Alvin's gentle, good-humored patience. No matter how difficult my demands, Alvin never took offense and never abandoned a project.

Alvin did not practice any one of the formal religions, but he was, I always felt, a profoundly religious person. He was always directly concerned with the essences of life. His theories of art went beyond technique to a wider concept of the way in which art could enrich our lives and give the pattern of society some meaning. I never knew anyone who had a more highly developed ethical sense. Recently I have been reading the Dhammapada, a collection of sayings of the Buddha, and so many of its truths bear testimony to Alvin's life. I would like to read you a few of them as we think of our friend and what he stood for.

Never in this world can hatred be stilled by hatred; it will be stilled only by non-hatred—this is the Law Eternal.

As a fletcher makes straight his arrow, so does the wise man make straight the mind which, trembling and unsteady, is difficult to guard and restrain.

The perfume of flowers cannot travel against the wind, be it the scent of sandal, tagara or jasmine, but the sweet odour of a good man travels even against the wind; the righteous pervade every place with their fragrance.

Though one should in battle conquer a thousand men a thousand times, he who conquers himself has the more glorious victory.

If one should find a wise companion with whom to consort, a man of good life and self-posessed, let one walk with him joyfully and deliberately, vanquishing all troubles.

Just as a man who has lived long abroad is met on this safe return from afar by kinsmen, friends and welcoming companions who come to greet him; so is the doer of good deeds, when he passes from this world to the next, welcomed by his good deeds as a dear kinsman returned home.

I should also like to read you a few lines from "The Way of Truth" of Lao Tzu. This was a poem that Alvin himself loved and perhaps it expresses something of his own belief.

What we look for beyond seeing
And call the unseen,
Listen for beyond hearing
And call the unheard,
Grasp for beyond reaching
And call the withheld,
All these merge beyond understanding

In a oneness

Which does not merely rise and give light,

Does not merely set and leave darkness,

But forever sends forth a succession of living

   things as mysterious

As the unbegotten existence to which they return.

One who is anciently aware of existence

Is master of every moment;

He feels no break since time beyond time

In the way life flows.

And another poet who Alvin liked was Dylan Thomas, who wrote, so movingly that "death shall have no dominion."

Dead men naked they shall be one

With the man in the wind and the west moon;

When their bones are picked clean and the

   clean bones gone,

They shall have stars at elbow and foot;

Though they go mad they shall be sane,

Though they sink through the sea they shall rise again;

Though lovers be lost love shall not;

And death shall have no dominion.

And then, as our last hail and farewell to our friend, I should like to adapt the lines of Robert Fitzgerald's translation of the poem which the Roman poet Catullus wrote on the death of his brother.

By strangers' coasts and waters, many days at sea,

We come here for the rights of your unworlding,

Bringing for you, the dead, these lasts gifts of the living

And our words—vain sounds for the man of dust.

Alas, our friend,

You have been taken from us. You have been taken

   from us,

By cold chance turned a shadow, and our pain.

Here are the foods of the old ceremony, appointed

Long ago for the starvelings under earth:

Take them; the tears of your friends have made them

   wet; and take

Into eternity our hail and farewell.

APPENDIX 2
PRÉCIS FOR A BOOK ON THE WORK OF ALVIN LUSTIG
May 31, 1955

[*Author's note: In response to a query from Harry Ford, an editor at Alfred A. Knopf, Lustig wrote this précis.*]

These pages roughly outline the editorial and pictorial contents of a book dealing with my activities in the field of design. Besides a selected cross section of my work it would contain a number of essays dealing with the theory and practice of design.

Editorially the contents would consist of a series of loosely related essays dealing with many aspects of design. The subjects would include such general themes as philosophical and esthetic attitudes, definitions of the role of the design in an industrial society, critical comments on various approaches, notes on design education, thoughts on specialization versus non-specialization, as well as specific discussions on such subjects as the organizing principles of design, a step-by-step analysis of the solution of a problem, methods of contemporary typography, principles of architectural lettering, and symbol and association in design. These essays would be more carefully developed versions of some of the lectures and teaching methods used by myself during the last few years. They would be connected by the over all theme of design but would differ in tone and level. Typographic presentation of these essays, especially in relation to pictorial material, might vary considerably.

The work shown would be a selection of commissioned pieces of typography and graphic design, architectural lettering, architecture, industrial and interior design. There would also be a number of projects and experiments some of which would be developed specially for this book.

The book should sell for approximately $10 retail and would be aimed primarily at the professional and student audience. It would range between 200 and 250 pages, written material counting for no more than one-third.

Physically, the book should be fairly large in format (approximately 9" x 12") and predominately pictorial in character. Rather than being the usual glossy paper presentation of work, which has become rather commonplace among art books, it would attempt to create an atmosphere of lively visual interest which would suggest a specific climate instead of being merely a record of work. Perhaps varying paper stocks would be used for change of pace and more than one type of printing process employed. A small amount of full color should be planned. This should be a fresh and exciting example of bookmaking itself. Careful planning in relation to production methods would make this possible, without running into excessive costs.

APPENDIX 3

[*Author's note: A request from Harry Ford prompted this letter on July 8, 1955, with a more detailed outline*].

Below I have attempted to be a bit more specific as to titles of essays and their contents. This is still a tentative list and I would not like to be held rigidly to it. However, it does reflect generally the subjects and approach that I plan to take.

Forward

This would be a personal statement expressing my belief in the need for the artist to be articulate and why this is especially so at this moment in our social history. It would set the tone for the essays and make clear that these are in the nature of personal commitments and are not offered in the spirit of polemics.

The Designer Living In Society

This would state my belief that the designer's role today is dual and somewhat ambivalent. He must be critical of the same society that he attempts to serve. The traditional role of the artist being no longer possible in an industrialized democracy, what are the values which he must affirm? What is the future of art in America? I would attempt to clarify my belief that the artist will only find salvation through some vital connection with the industrial process despite the dangers of depersonalization and mechanization that are inherent within it. The regenerative formative process in which the design is involved would be emphasized.

Structure And The Sense Of Order

This essay would attempt to define the structural sense which is inherent in our contemporary thinking and which underlies the entire formative process of our time and which distinguishes it from traditional concepts. Some references would be made to Lancelot Law Whyte and his scientific counterpart of concepts which still remain intuitive for the artist. There would be emphasis on the sense of process and formation rather than on fixed and final form which only varies stylistically as in the past. This essay would seek to penetrate rather deeply into a new concept of values which already has a scientific and aesthetic justification and which could be extended quite validly into the moral and religious area.

Private And Public Symbols

This essay would attempt to define the nature of the symbolic transformation that is taking place in our society and the difference of disciplines that are required of the artist as opposed to the designer. The designer is primarily concerned with the public symbol and the personal vision can only indirectly have meaning for him. The artist in the more traditional sense, and by traditional we mean the immediate past, is primarily concerned with the personal symbol or vision. The interplay between these two attitudes and the differences of orientation they require will be explored.

Design Education

This would be a combination of an objective analysis of the different attitudes now existing and their limitations. Followed by a purely personal projection of an approach to design education. It would deal with such subjects as specialization versus non-specialization, more decisions that face the graduate, the problem of experience and orientation towards a fluid society.

Scale And Environment

This would attempt to define the nature of visual relationships when seen on the cityscape or landscape scale. It would seek to define the nature of the physical environment that an industrial society will have to develop in terms of human needs. This essay would also explore the new character of relationships that will start to develop between painting, sculpture, landscape and architecture as industrial democracy defines itself more clearly.

Principles Of Contemporary Typography

Very general attitudes rather than fixed rules would be stated in this essay. An effort would be made to pin point those points of view which are beyond fashion and whim and form the solid basis of contemporary typography. Axis relationships, scale, weight, principles of display, psychological emphasis would all be discussed as well as an analysis of the conflicting attitudes which still exist within the body of contemporary typography.

An Approach To Architectural Lettering

This is a field in which very little technical material exists and as the author has gained some reputation as a specialist in this field a discussion of the subject would be appropriate. This essay would be based on a lecture given at the Museum of Modern Art and would use some of the visual material prepared for the talk. Primarily it would seek to point out those points of contact and divergence that exist in the design organizing principles of contemporary architecture and lettering. It would show why historic relationships were valid for their time but are not any longer appropriate for today.

In the letter I sent to Sidney [Jacobs, production manager of Knopf] I had allowed for approximately sixty pages of text including the forwards, which allows about a little less than eight pages for an essay, which sounds about right.

I hope this is all specific enough for you, and I look forward to hearing from you.

[*Author's note: On July 28, 1955, Sidney Jacobs responded: "Dear Alvin, I am completely confounded by the mathematics of your précis for the book you propose to do. Let me break it down into its easiest and simplest terms so far as printing and reproduction is concerned and raise the questions as I go along." He proceeds to indicate in great detail the various possible specifications from jacket to interior. It seemed as though the book was going to go forward. However, that was the last piece of correspondence between Knopf and Lustig.*]

1 Alvin Lustig, "Alvin Lustig: About the Career of a Young Man With an Inquiring Mind," *Interiors*, September 1946.

2 Claire Imrie, "Alvin Lustig: A Versatile Designer," *American Artist*, November 1952.

3 R. Holland Melson, *Collected Writings*. (Alvin Lustig Fund, Yale University, New Haven, 1958).

4 C. F. O. Clarke, "Alvin Lustig: Cover Designs," *Graphis*, vol. 1, no. 23, 1948.

5 Alvin Lustig, unpublished notes, undated. Collection of Elaine Lustig Cohen.

6 Alvin Lustig, "Personal Notes on Design," *American Institute of Graphic Arts Journal*, April 1955.

7 Alvin Lustig, "California: The Cultural Frontier," *Western Advertising*, June 1943.

8 Alvin Lustig, unpublished essay, undated. Collection of Elaine Lustig Cohen.

9 R. Holland Melson, "Alvin Lustig: The Designer as Teacher," *Print XXIII*, January/February 1969.

10 Alvin Lustig to James Laughlin, undated. The Houghton Library, Bequest James Laughlin IV (Correspondence, 1943–1955 and undated).

11 Alvin Lustig, "Alvin Lustig: About the Career of a Young Man With an Inquiring Mind," *Interiors*, September 1946.

12 Alvin Lustig to Estelle Laverne, December 22, 1954. Collection Archives of American Art.

13 Ward Ritchie, "Fine Printing: The Los Angeles Tradition." Washington: Library of Congress, 1987.

14 David Davies, "The Graphic Art of Alvin Lustig," unpublished manuscript, 1983. Copy in the Collection of Elaine Lustig Cohen.

15 Alvin Lustig, "Design, A Process of Teaching," in *Collected Writings*, R. Holland Melson, ed. (Alvin Lustig Fund, Yale University, New Haven, 1958).

16 David Davies, op. cit.

17 Elaine Lustig Cohen in email to author, 2004.

18 David Davies, op. cit.

19 Ward Ritchie to David Davies. Date unknown.

20 Ward Ritchie to David Davies. Date unknown.

21 David Davies, op. cit.

22 Alvin Lustig, "Personal Notes on Design," in *Selected Writings*, op. cit.

23 Alvin Lustig to Laughlin, undated. The Houghton Library, Bequest James Laughlin IV (Correspondence, 1943–1955 and undated).

24 Alvin Lustig to Laughlin. January 9, 1948. The Houghton Library, Bequest James Laughlin IV (Correspondence, 1943–1955 and undated).

25 Ward Ritchie, *A Tale of Two Books*, Los Angeles: Richard J. Hoffman, 1985.

26 Ward Ritchie to Elaine Lustig Cohen, November 1982. Collection of Elaine Lustig Cohen.

27 William Everson response to promotional mailing from Ward Ritchie, undated. Collection of Elaine Lustig Cohen.

28 Ward Ritchie to Elaine Lustig Cohen, November 1982. Collection of Elaine Lustig Cohen.

29 James Laughlin, "The Book Jackets of Alvin Lustig," *Print*, Oct/Nov 1956.

30 David Davies, op. cit.

31 Alvin Lustig, untitled essay. *Book Jackets by Alvin Lustig*. New York: Gotham Book Mart, 1947.

32 James Laughlin, "The Book Jackets of Alvin Lustig," *Print*, Oct/Nov 1956.

33 Arthur A. Cohen, "A Book Publisher Uses Graphic Design," typescript for article published under the title "Book Design" in *Art in America*, no. 4, 1959.

34 James Laughlin, "The Book Jackets of Alvin Lustig," *Print*, Oct/Nov 1956.

35 Alvin Lustig to James Laughlin. January 9, 1948. The Houghton Library, Bequest James Laughlin IV (Correspondence, 1943-1955 and undated).

36 C. F. O. Clarke, op. cit.

37 Alvin Lustig, "Contemporary Book Design," *Design Quarterly*, no. 31, 1954.

38 Alvin Lustig, "Personal Notes on Design," op. cit.

39 James Laughlin to Alvin Lustig, February 14, 1951. The Houghton Library, Bequest James Laughlin IV (Correspondence, 1943-1955 and undated).

40 Alvin Lustig to James Laughlin. Unsigned and undated. The Houghton Library, Bequest James Laughlin IV (Correspondence, 1943-1955 and undated).

41 James Laughlin to Alvin Lustig, September 2, 1948. The Houghton Library, Bequest James Laughlin IV (Correspondence, 1943-1955 and undated).

42 Ibid.

43 James Laughlin to Alvin Lustig, undated. The Houghton Library, Bequest James Laughlin IV (Correspondence, 1943–1955 and undated).

44 Alvin Lustig to James Laughlin, undated. The Houghton Library, Bequest James Laughlin IV (Correspondence, 1943–1955 and undated).

45 Alvin Lustig to James Laughlin, c. 1940. The Houghton Library, Bequest James Laughlin IV (Correspondence, 1943–1955 and undated).

46 Alvin Lustig to James Laughlin, undated. The Houghton Library, Bequest James Laughlin IV (Correspondence, 1943–1955 and undated).

47 John Lee to Harlan Logan, December 7, 1943. Collection of Elaine Lustig Cohen.

48 Alvin Lustig to James Laughlin, December 26, 1943. The Houghton Library, Bequest James Laughlin IV (Correspondence, 1943–1955 and undated).

49 Alvin Lustig to James Laughlin, undated. The Houghton Library, Bequest James Laughlin IV (Correspondence, 1943–1955 and undated).

50 Alvin Lustig to James Laughlin, undated. The Houghton Library, Bequest James Laughlin IV (Correspondence, 1943–1955 and undated).

51 Alvin Lustig, "Formal Values in Trademark Design," in *Seven Designers Look at Trademark Design*, Egbert Jacobson, ed. Chicago: Paul Theobald, 1952.

52 Alvin Lustig, "Formal Values in Trademark Design," op. cit.

53 Alvin Lustig, "Formal Values in Trademark Design," op. cit.

54 Monte Factor to Alvin Lustig, 1954. Collection Archives of American Art.

55 Alvin Lustig to Monte Factor, 1954. Collection Archives of American Art.

56 "Northland Shopping Center," *Architectural Forum*, June 1954.

57 Alvin Lustig, notes for "Outline for an Integrated Design Program," c. 1954. Collection of Elaine Lustig Cohen.

58 Jane Thompson, interview with the author for *I.D. magazine*, reprinted in *Design Literacy* by Steven Heller and Karen Pomeroy, Allworth Press, 1997.

59 Jane Thompson, ibid.

60 Arthur A. Cohen, "A Book Publisher Uses Graphic Design," typescript for article titled "Book Design" in *Art in America*, no. 4, 1959.

61 Arthur A. Cohen, ibid.

62 Alvin Lustig, undated notes. Collection of Elaine Lustig Cohen.

63 "The Lustig Portfolio," *Interiors*, June 1953.

64 Ibid.

65 Ibid.

66 "Alvin Lustig Design Offices for Reporter Publications," *Architectural Forum*, May 1946.

67 "An Artist's Own House, New York," Architectural Design, April 1953. Originally appeared in *Domus*, November 1952.

68 Elaine Lustig Cohen, conversation with the author, 2004.

69 Walter Landor to Alvin Lustig, September 28, 1948. Collection of Elaine Lustig Cohen.

70 Alvin Lustig, "California Modern," *Design*, October 1947.

71 Jules Langsner, undated draft for unpublished essay, c. late 1940s. Collection Archives of American Art.

72 Alvin Lustig to James Laughlin, undated. The Houghton Library, Bequest James Laughlin IV (Correspondence, 1943–1955 and undated).

73 Alvin Lustig, "California Modern," op. cit.

74 Alvin Lustig, "Design and the Idea," *Western Advertising*, June 1943.

75 William H. Thomas, quoted in memorial for Alvin Lustig, 1955.

76 Alvin Lustig, notes for an untitled speech, September 1953. Collection of Elaine Lustig Cohen.

77 Alvin Lustig, "Modern Printed Fabrics," *American Fabrics*, Winter 1951.

78 Erwin Laverne to Alvin Lustig, July 27, 1949. Collection of Elaine Lustig Cohen.

79 Alvin Lustig, notes for an untitled essay, September 1953. Collection of Elaine Lustig Cohen.

80 Alvin Lustig to James Laughlin, October 21, 1950. The Houghton Library, Bequest James Laughlin IV (Correspondence, 1943–1955 and undated).

81 Hortense Mendel to Alvin Lustig, July 19, 1949. Collection of Elaine Lustig Cohen.

82 Alvin Lustig, instructions for installation, 1950. Collection of Elaine Lustig Cohen.

83 Hortense Mendel letter to Alvin Lustig, June 22, 1949. Collection of Elaine Lustig Cohen.

84 Alvin Lustig to "Pat" (last name unknown; she briefly worked in Lustig's office), undated. Collection of Elaine Lustig Cohen.

85 Ibid.

86 Alvin Lustig to William De Mayo, November 18, 1954. Collection of Elaine Lustig Cohen.

87 Helen Reid to Alvin Lustig, October 16, 1950. Collection of Elaine Lustig Cohen.

88 Alvin Lustig, draft for "Design, a Process of Teaching," *Western Arts Association Bulletin*, vol. 26, no. 4, September 1952. Collection of Elaine Lustig Cohen.

89 R. Holland Melson, "Alvin Lustig: The Designer as Teacher," *Print XXIII*, January/February 1969.

90 Alvin Lustig, "Design, a Process of Teaching," *Western Arts Association Bulletin*, vol. 26, no. 4, September 1952.

91 Alvin Lustig, "Graphic Design," Collected Writings, R. Holland Melson, ed. (Alvin Lustig Fund, Yale University, New Haven, 1958).

92 Josef Albers to Alvin Lustig, August 30, 1945. Collection of Elaine Lustig Cohen.

93 Alvin Lustig to James Laughlin, undated. The Houghton Library, Bequest James Laughlin IV (Correspondence, 1943–1955 and undated).

94 Alvin Lustig, "Design, a Process of Teaching," *Western Arts Association Bulletin*, vol. 26, no. 4, September 1952.

95 Ibid.

96 Alvin Lustig to James Laughlin, undated. The Houghton Library, Bequest James Laughlin IV (Correspondence, 1943-1955 and undated).

97 Eugene Weston, personal correspondence with the author.

98 Alvin Lustig, "Design, a Process of Teaching," op. cit.

99 Peter Dodge, personal correspondence with Elaine Lustig Cohen, 2006.

100 Alvin Lustig, "Design, a Process of Teaching," op. cit.

101 R. Holland Melson, op. cit.

102 Alvin Lustig, "Design Program for the University of Georgia," in *Collected Writings*, R. Holland Melson, ed. (Alvin Lustig Fund, Yale University, New Haven, 1958).

103 Ibid.

104 Ibid.

105 Ibid.

106 Ibid.

107 Alvin Lustig, "Graphic Design," *Design*, 1946.

108 Alvin Lustig, "Design, a Process of Teaching," op. cit.

109 Alvin Lustig, unpublished essay, undated. Collection of Elaine Lustig Cohen.

110 Alvin Lustig, unpublished notes, response to an article in *House Beautiful* magazine, undated. Collection Archives of American Art.

111 Alvin Lustig, unpublished notes, undated. Collection of Elaine Lustig Cohen.

ACKNOWLEDGMENTS

I am deeply indebted to my friend Steven Heller and his early interest in the work of Alvin Lustig and his knowledge and commitment to the field of design and its relationship to society. His dedication has made this work possible.

Thanks are also due to Roger Remington and Barbara J. Hodik whose book *Nine Pioneers in American Graphic Design* helped to revive the interest in Lustig in 1989.

Special thanks to Greg D'Onofrio and Patricia Belen who convinced me to have them create a Lustig web site which they executed with loving care. Thanks to Douglas Clouse and Rita James, who made an enormous contribution with their Alvin Lustig exhibition for the Bard Graduate Center in 2007.

Over the years my friends at New Directions Books have continued to appreciate the Lustig designs and are presently reviving some of the original New Classic covers. I am grateful for the number of designers who continued a small underground of interest and to the current group of young designers who have rediscovered him. I want to express my love and appreciation to my daughter, Tamar Cohen, for her incredible design of the book.

Also, I would like to thank the many designers, students, friends and writers who have kept the Lustig image alive over the past half century: Ward Ritchie, David Davies, Peter Dodge, June Wayne, Richard de Natale, Mildred Constantine, Eugene Weston, Frederick Usher.

Finally, much gratitude goes to Susan Lustig Peck, Patricia Peck Nocella and Amelia Peck for providing needed background material and rare photographs of the young Alvin.

—Elaine Lustig Cohen

This book would have been impossible if not for the generosity and knowledge of my collaborator and friend, Elaine Lustig Cohen. Over the years she has not only allowed free access to all the materials for this book, but also for many of my other books. I am deeply indebted to Elaine.

Thanks to Alan Rapp, former editor at Chronicle Books, who acquired this project. He had long been a staunch advocate of design history and criticism, and I missed not working with him on this volume. Yet I was fortunate that his replacement was Michelle Dunn Marsh, who enthusiastically shepherded this manuscript from beginning to end. Thanks also to Bridget Watson Payne and Michael Morris at Chronicle for their key participation in the final product.

Tamar Cohen, thank YOU! She gave form and beauty to this work. Her design is everything we wanted and more.

Appreciation to Rick Poynor and John Walters of EYE, Hans Dieter Riechert of Baseline and Marty Fox and Joyce Rutter Kaye of PRINT magazines for publishing earlier articles on Alvin Lustig that were adapted as texts for this book.

And thanks to Rober Dirig, College Archivist, Art Center College of Design, for the photographs on pages 120 and 185.

Finally, thanks to Louis Danziger, Ivan Chermayeff and Milton Glaser for words of wisdom.

—Steven Heller